W9-BXX-771

Other books available from Sure Foundation:

Life's Ultimate Privilege
Ultimate Intention
Unto Full Stature
A Hive of Busy Bees
Another Hive of Busy Bees
Seeing God's Wisdom
Seeing God's Purpose

Larger Window
© Copyright 2002 Sure Foundation

Published by Sure Foundation
8905 Kingston Pike Suite 12-316, Knoxville, TN 37923
Master Press website: www.master-press.com
1-800-325-9136

Distributed by Master Press

SF 936595-13-2

Printed in the United States of America.

DeVern Fromke

Stories That Open God's
Larger
Window

Sure Foundation
8905 Kingston Pike Suite 12-316
Knoxville, TN 37923

THIS SELECTION OF STORIES

is primarily focused toward readers who have become

.... discouraged with life and its down-side, or
.... disappointed with their church fellowship, or
.... disillusioned with their understanding of the Bible, or
.... defeated in their lack of spiritual development, or
.... devastated by some unexpected circumstance.

It is hoped these stories will help you understand some of the most basic lessons in the Bible as it unfolds God's grace, mercy, peace and fulfillment. We recall how Jesus used many parables to teach the multitude, because His listeners could better grasp real life-issues from His word-pictures. It is for this same reason we choose the following stories.

Many who have read some of our earlier books will perhaps expect similar teaching lessons developing spiritual maturity.

I ask you to lay aside all your expectations and recognize that the unique purpose of **THIS BOOK** is focused to enlighten and encourage the hurting, wounded and hopeless—those five kinds of readers we have listed above.

The author

An Amazing Difference

OVER thirty years ago my wife and I moved to an 80 acre rural setting away from the hustle of Indianapolis. It was almost immediately that we realized the need to enlarge our small house, which had one tiny window on the west side. By building a large room to the west side we were able to add a large window (7 ft. by 24 ft.) giving us an amazing overview. Words can hardly explain what a delightful change this made to our living quarters.

We remember that many who entered our house stood with breathless amazement: "Wow, this opens up a new world." It really did! It was awesome to behold the lovely valley below, to look down on the grassy meadow, to observe the variety of trees and sometimes watch deer and other wild animals as they would frolic in their natural freedom.

The elderly couple who sold us this place had lived there for over fifty years. For them to leave this house they had built with their own hands was heart-wrenching, and together we wept many tears as they moved from this awesome valley-setting they had enjoyed so much in their lifetime.

What still baffles me, however, is that someone could live so long with such a limited outlook upon the beauty around them. They had one small window over the kitchen sink! Of course there were other small windows on the other sides, but only one small window to the west looking out over the beautiful valley. Can you imagine spending a lifetime with one small window, when all of God's glorious creation was available to enjoy!

When I reflect on them, I realize there are countless millions of God's children whose viewpoint is also confined to their small window. I am not speaking now of a physical window, but of their contentedness with a small spiritual vision.

You have recognized by now that these stories are being placed in sequence to unfold the enlarging aspects of God's grace, mercy and peace. Along with this, we are recognizing how God is continually working in our lives to move us from being merely...

...objects of His grace...to BECOME GRACE-GIVERS,
...objects of His mercy...to BECOME MERCIFUL,
...objects of His peace, to BECOME PEACE-MAKERS.

While we are always needing to experience more of God's grace, mercy and peace working in our lives, what God has planned and purposed to accomplish through us should become primary.

We believe this was the deepest concern in the Apostle Paul's prayer for the Ephesian saints: *"...the eyes of your understanding being enlightened; that ye may know what is the hope of HIS calling...the riches of the glory of HIS inheritance in the saints."* Earlier in the chapter Paul has reminded them of their inheritance, but now He presses them to move beyond that smaller window (of their inheritance) to recognize THE LARGER WINDOW: what God will get—"His inheritance in them."

We will show how God, from the beginning, has invited us to sit with Him and see His unfolding PURPOSE FOR HIMSELF, and then for us to understand how we relate to that Master Plan. It will also become evident that Our Father has planned for His Son, Jesus Christ, to become the Divine Centerpiece of all things.

When we grasp the importance of this Divine Centerpiece, and what it really means, (how as members of Christ's body we are also included), then the final glory that God receives will also be a shared glory. Our Father can only be wholly satisfied when we are truly satisfied. That is the essence of "glorifying God and enjoying Him forever." Once we grasp this we shall move from our man-centered pre-occupation with what we get, to become wholly occupied with the glory that God will get from our lives. Finally, this book is a call to each of us to move from our narrow window to re-interpret everything and enjoy the awesome wonder of...

GOD'S LARGER WINDOW

Seasons of Unfolding Awareness

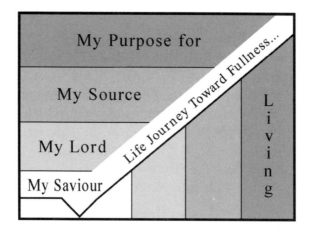

Let us consider the four seasons we will pass through in our journey toward fulfilling God's Purpose for our lives.

(1) You will recall that day when you bowed before Lord Jesus and acknowledged you were a sinner, needing a Savior. Your faith reached out to trust His finished work for you on Calvary. Since then it has taken much time (perhaps a life-time) to recognize all that was included in your salvation. To more fully understand all that is included in salvation will be an UNFOLDING AWARE-NESS.

(2) If you were properly instructed, you were told that Jesus was not only your Savior, but He would also become your Lord. Someone has described this: you are now under new management with a new boss. The discovery of all His Lordship means in every aspect of your walk, will become an UNFOLDING AWARENESS.

(3) More than 40 years ago I wrote on the back fly-leaf of my Bible: "I never knew He was all I needed until He was all I had." I felt sure then that I knew just a bit of what that meant. Yet, I have been forced to admit since: "only the bitter realities of life could have crowded me to know Him more and more as my Source." The Psalmist explained: "...all my springs are in Thee," because he had discovered the bottom of his own empty well. To

understand how the Lord Jesus is my all-sufficient Source will also become an UNFOLDING AWARENESS.

(4) Finally, we come to the fourth season when we uncover the great WHY of all things. What plans did God have on His great drafting board "before the foundation of the world"? Until we really understand this eternal purpose of the Father for HIMSELF, we cannot appreciate how Jesus as Savior, Lord and Source, finds its full focus in this Purpose.

Remember, only as we understand what the Father has purposed for Himself, can we appreciate God's Larger Window—THE CENTRAL THEME of this book.

The Larger Window of Grace

Awakening Grace **BEFORE** Titus 2:11 Psalms 84:11	Saving Grace **WHEN** Eph. 2:8-9 Rom 3:24	Growing Grace **AS** 2 Pet. 3:18 Eph. 1:7, 2:7	Special Grace **BECAUSE** Gen. 6:8 Exod. 33:12-17

Four Aspects of His Manifold Grace

AWAKENING grace... God has been working in our lives BEFORE we are really aware of His dealing. It is this awakening grace that opens blind eyes, softens hardened hearts and creates desire and need to trust Him as lord and receive His substitutionary work on the cross. We shall see how God's common grace has been open to all in these first stories.

SAVING grace... Many who have been exposed to Biblical truths have acknowledged they had heard about Jesus as Savior of the world, and had even assumed this included them. Then the moment of enlightenment came WHEN "the light of the gospel" broke in and they realized how helpless and hopeless as lost sinners they were. For the first time they needed Someone who could pay their sin-debt and give them eternal life. WHEN they believed, His saving grace became very personal and they could begin to sing with all God's children... "amazing grace how sweet the sound!"

GROWING grace... As we proceed in this new and living way, we discover our initial trust must become a daily trusting. We begin to realize God has not called us to an easy way, yet it can become a most blessed way AS we discover He is our total Source for every difficult situation. So we can only grow in grace AS we learn to draw from His river of grace (supply).

SPECIAL grace... comes in abounding measure BECAUSE God selects a vessel for some distinctive purpose. This special grace is uniquely available to those whom God has chosen to use as a demonstration: Noah found (special) grace; Daniel found grace in the lion's den; his three companions found grace in the fiery furnace; Jonah, Job, Moses—each found special grace BECAUSE God selected them to be a demonstration of grace according to His divine purpose. Never assume that you could go through such a difficult ordeal apart from receiving God's special grace.

Oh the riches and the glory of His manifold grace!

God Knows Your Number

EVANGELIST KEN GAUB
PONDERS TO HIMSELF, as he and his family were traveling in their Silver Eagle bus: "God, sometimes I wonder if you know where I am." At that moment a melancholy cloud of self-pity enshrouded my mind. My hands tensed their grip on the steering wheel, and I stared through the windshield of the bus. I seemed to have used up all my faith in ministering to others. "Lord, even a preacher needs to know that you are aware of him once in a while," I said to myself.

"Hey, Dad, let's get some pizza." The voice of my younger son Dan stirred me out of my self-induced cocoon of despondency. My wife Barbara and daughter Becki agreed with Dan. It had been a long day and was way past time to eat.

We exited from I-75 and turned onto Route 741 just south of Dayton, Ohio. Bright, colorful signs advertising a wide variety of fast food restaurants were a welcome sight. Satisfied murmurs arose behind me as we sighted the local pizza parlor.

As I maneuvered the big Silver Eagle bus into the parking lot, Dan and Becki were already clamoring to get out and into the restaurant. Barbara stood at the bottom step and turned to wait for me. I sat staring into space. "Aren't you coming, Ken?" she asked.

"Naw, I'm not really hungry," I replied. "You go ahead with the kids. I need to stretch out and unwind a bit."

I moved back into the living room area to the sofa, folded my arms behind my head, leaned back to think. 'It really is a beautiful day,' I thought as I glanced out the window. 'Maybe I should get some fresh air.'

I stepped outside, closed the bus doors and looked around. Then as I saw a Dairy Queen down the street I thought, 'maybe I'm thirsty.'

After purchasing a coke, I strolled in the direction of the bus. The impatient ringing of a telephone somewhere up the street jarred me out of my doldrums. It was coming from a phone booth at a service station on the corner. As I approached it continued its ringing.

I paused and looked to see if anyone was going to answer the phone. Noise from the traffic flowing through the busy intersection must have drowned out the sound because the service station attendant continued looking after his customers, oblivious to the incessant ringing.

Why doesn't someone answer that phone? I wondered. The ringing continued. I began reasoning, it may be important. What if it's an emergency?

I started to walk away, but curiosity overcame my indifference. I stepped inside the booth and picked up the phone. "Hello," I said casually and took a big sip of coke.

The operator whined, "Long distance call for Ken Gaub."

My eyes widened and I almost choked on a chunk of ice from my coke. Swallowing hard I said, "You're crazy." Realizing I shouldn't speak to an operator like that I added, "This can't be! I was just walking down the street not bothering anyone, and the phone was ringing..."

The operator ignored my crude explanation and asked once more, "Is Ken Gaub there? I have a long distance call for him."

It took a moment to gain control of my babbling, but I finally replied, "Yes, he is." Searching for a possible explanation, I suddenly had the answer. "I know what this is! I'm on candid camera!"

While trying to locate the hidden camera, I reached up and tried to smooth my hair. I wanted to look my best for those millions of television viewers. Stepping outside the phone booth and looking quickly in every direction, the telephone cord nearly broke as I stretched it to its limit. I couldn't find a camera anywhere! Impatiently, the operator interrupted again, "I have a long distance call for Ken Gaub. Is he there?"

Still shaken as well as perplexed, I asked, "How in the world can this be? How did you reach me here? I was walking down the street... the pay phone started ringing, and I decided to answer it." My voice grew louder in the excitement. "I just answered it on a chance. You can't mean me. This is impossible!"

"Well," the operator asked, "is Mr. Gaub there or isn't he?" The tone of her voice convinced me the call was real and that her patience was at a limit.

I then replied,"Yes, he is. I'm he."

She was not convinced "Are you sure?" she asked.

Flustered, I half-jokingly replied, "As far as I know at this point, I am" and I heard another voice say, "Yes, that's him, operator. I believe that's him."

I listened dumfounded to a strange voice identify herself. The caller blurted, "Ken Gaub, I'm Millie from Harrisburg,

Pennsylvania. You don't know me, but I'm desperate. Please help me."

"What can I do for you?" I responded.

She began weeping. I waited until she had regained control, and then she continued. "I'm about to commit suicide, and I just finished writing a note. While writing it, I began to pray and tell God I really didn't want to do this. I suddenly remembered seeing you on television and thought if I could just talk to you, you could help me. I knew that was impossible because I didn't know how to reach you, and I didn't know anyone who could help me find you. I continued writing my suicide note because I could see no way out of my situation. As I wrote, numbers came to my mind and I scribbled them down."

At this point she began weeping again, and I prayed silently for wisdom to help her.

She continued. "I looked at the numbers and thought, 'Wouldn't it be wonderful if I had a miracle from God and He had given me Ken's phone number?' I decided to try calling it. I figured it was worth the chance. It really was! I can't believe I'm talking to you. Are you in your office in California?

I replied "Lady, I don't have an office in California. My office is in Yakima, Washington."

A little surprised, she asked, "Oh really, then where are you?"

"Don't you know?" I responded. "You made the call."

She explained, "But I don't even know what area I'm calling. I just dialed the number that I had on this paper."

I told her "Ma'am, you won't believe this, but I'm in a phone booth near Dayton, Ohio!"

"Really?" She exclaimed, "Well, what are you doing there?"

I kidded her gently, "Well, I'm answering the phone. It was ringing as I walked by, so I answered it."

Knowing this encounter could only have been arranged by God, I began to counsel the woman. As she told me of her despair and frustration, the presence of the Holy Spirit flooded the phone booth giving me words of wisdom beyond my ability. In a matter of moments she prayed the sinner's prayer and met the One who would lead her out of her situation into a new life.

I walked away from that telephone booth with an electrifying sense of our heavenly Father's concern for each of His children. I was astounded as I thought of the astronomical odds of this happening. With all the millions of phones and innumerable combinations of numbers, only an all-knowing God could have caused that woman to call that number in that phone booth at that moment in time. (KG)

Ken Gaub was calling for reassurance
Millie was calling for help
Since the Fall in the garden, God has been calling all men to repentance.

---

* In this almost unbelievable story we recognize three who are calling: A tired, and weary Ken Gaub is inwardly calling out to God for reassurance that He is effective in his ministry.

* In her dark hour of despair Millie is calling out to God. We must recognize she is not merely voicing a prayer of need, Millie is "crying out" in desperation with a heart that must not be denied. The good news is that God hears such a "cry"; the Scriptures record how often God responds to such a whole-hearted desperate cry for help.

* Next, it is important for us to know that God is the First Caller. Ever since Adam's departure in the Garden to go his own way, God has been calling every member of Adam's family back to Himself. When the Psalmist explains: "Deep calls unto deep," he is describing the Eternal Spirit of God that is calling out to each human spirit. One translator explains it: "Deep Calls unto deep, at the call of the Fountainhead." Yes, God is THE Fountainhead, who has uniquely designed each of us with an inner room (our spirit) that He made for Himself. God is calling to remind us that He not only will forgive our sins, but He wants to come to indwell our spirit, i.e. to reside within us. Finally we must recognize: God continues calling each of us to that Divine fulfillment He has planned for each life.

As we progress in these stories, it will become increasingly evident that we will find no real meaning in life until we yield ourselves to God that He might "make home" within us. I trust you may soon realize that this book has come into your hands perhaps through another (by God's direction).

God is calling You to Himself. He has been calling you for a long time. This could be your day for responding to His call:

"Today, if You will hear (My) His voice...(And...)
Whosoever shall call upon the name of the Lord, shall be saved."

Yes, FATHER, deep inside of me I hear Your voice... and I do say... "yes."

15

God Knows Your Blindness

BILLY GRAHAM EXPLAINS. . .
HOW GOD demonstrated His faithfulness to a wife who was having her faith tested by a difficult and bitter husband.

This story is about a mother in an African nation who came to Christ, and grew strong in her commitment and devotion to the Lord. As so often happens, however, this alienated her from her husband, who over the years came to despise and hate her new devotion to Christ.

His anger and bitterness reached a climax when he decided to kill his wife, their two children and himself, unable to live in such self-inflicted misery. But he needed a motive. He decided that he would accuse her of stealing his precious keys—the keys to his bank, the house, and the car. Early one afternoon he left his bank and headed for the tavern. His route took him across a footbridge extended over the headwaters of the Nile River. For a moment he paused above the river and then dropped the keys. He spent all afternoon drinking and carousing at the local tavern.

Later that afternoon, his wife went to the fish market to buy the evening meal. She purchased a large Nile perch. As she was gutting the fish, to her astonishment, in its belly were her husband's keys. How had they gotten there? What were the circumstances? She did not know, but she cleaned them up and hung them on the hook.

When the young banker came home that night, exceedingly drunk and pounded open the front door he shouted, "Woman, where are my keys?" Already in bed, she got up, picked them off the hook in the bedroom, and handed them to her husband. When he saw the keys, by his own testimony he immediately became sober. He fell on his knees sobbing, asking for forgiveness, and confessed Jesus Christ as his Lord and Savior and was instantly converted. • (B.G.)

> PREVENIENT GRACE IS GOD'S DEALING IN US
> BEFORE WE RECOGNIZE OR RESPOND TO
> HIS CALLING FOR OUR LIFE.

God knows the deception and darkness of every heart before the light of salvation breaks in. This young banker is typical of the

16

blindness that prevails in any heart that walks in his own wilfulness. How much of the gospel message had he known? We do not know! We do know that night He was confronted with a Person (a Power greater than his selfishness) and He was willing to bow the knee and acknowledge Him as Lord.

It would be interesting to know how long this wife had prayed, or how long her church fellowship had interceded for this husband's salvation. We do know that God in His faithfulness answered in a most sovereign way. He had been watching the young banker–like a struggling fish on His line–waiting for the right moment to unveil His wondrous grace. So He directed a fish to receive those keys–and directed a wife to buy that very fish. How could he any longer resist when he found his "lost" keys on the nail at home. The Apostle Paul explains it: (Rom. 2:4)

"...despisest thou the riches of his goodness and forbearance
and longsuffering; not knowing that the goodness of God
leadeth thee to repentance?"

Would you believe our great Creator not only can make, but He can also direct His creatures to the right place... to fulfill His purpose.

... He directed a fish to pick up and then vomit Jonah on shore.

... He directed a fish to Peter's hook so both Peter and Jesus could pay their tax.

... He directed fish into the net of weary fishermen who had caught nothing in their long night of fishing.

... He directed this Nile perch to retrieve the set of keys which this frustrated young banker had thrown away.

It is possible someone now reading these lines is facing some crisis or some impossible situation. I would urge you now to honestly open your heart to God, (and perhaps to some trusted friend). You can call out to God for His intervention. Remember, God eagerly waits to demonstrate His goodness when You will call for His help. Though the Bible stories of Jonah and Peter may seem unbelievable, yet they actually happened! God waits to help you in your time of need.

MY FATHER, I do believe You are just as concerned for me as You were for this young wife and for her rebellious husband. What You did for them, You will do for me...yes, for anyone who is reading these lines.

God Knows Your Deepest Need

WE ARE NOT TOLD WHY,
but for months he had planned to murder the Queen. Slipping undetected into her bedroom, he hid in the mammoth walnut wardrobe. Covered by a velvet gown inside, he rehearsed his plan once more. He would know when the Queen had retired, because her maid-in-waiting would bid her goodnight and leave her room.

There was a crack in the wardrobe door which kept him from suffocating among the thicknesses of her gowns. Through it, he would be able to see when the Queen blew out the candle beside her bed. He would listen for her breathing to change, slip out quietly in his stocking feet, walk to the bed, and rid England of her Queen.

The rehearsing of his plan put him at ease. He leaned back inside the boards of the ornately carved wardrobe to wait. It could be some time before the Queen would enter the room to retire.

Then suddenly the door of the wardrobe opened and a huge hand, fingers spread open wide touched him. The groping hand immediately grabbed him by the shirt. In all of his planning the assassin had forgotten one thing: the Queen's room was thoroughly searched each night before she went to bed. As he was wrenched from seclusion, he dropped to his knees and began to plead with the Queen that she might extend grace to him.

"Sir, if I extend unto you my grace, what do you promise for the future?"

With the keenness of a theologian, the man answered, "Your Majesty, your Majesty, a grace that propositions and a grace that bargains is no grace at all!"

Queen Elizabeth recognized the truth of the man's bold response. She announced, "Yes, freely, by my grace, I forgive you."

Such grace freely given to the unworthy and undeserving often has the desired effect: it not only won him, but conquered his heart. From that moment the would-be assassin became the most devoted servant the Queen ever had.

We are not told why this disgruntled man determined to murder his Queen. We only know that through her guidance and grace, she had uncovered his deepest need and led him to a new purpose for living.

I would like to believe that Queen Elizabeth understood man's deepest need when she wanted a promise for his future. Her growth in wisdom had convinced her that every man needed some purpose bigger than himself to which he could give himself. Also the wise Queen knew that grace and purpose should never be separated.

History seems to indicate that Elizabeth was one of England's wisest and most godly Queens. If she knew her Bible, and we believe she did, she understood what the Apostle Paul meant when he wrote:

"God called each of us with a holy calling."
"We are the called according to His purpose and grace."

Of course, Queen Elizabeth could only offer this servant an extension of temporal life, while our God alone can offer us eternal life in Christ Jesus.

From this story I wish to introduce the main thesis of this book: All of us need forgiveness because we have (like Adam in the garden) turned to our own way... we are sinners. We have already considered how God offered forgiveness to Millie when she called, to the young banker when he bowed in repentance, and now forgiveness was granted to this assassin. This is God's amazing grace and goodness.

From the beginning God planned a way to rescue man from his fallen, sinful condition. As we see in the picture, it was God's intention that Adam would move along the race-course to fulfill the purpose God planned. (A to Z). In no way did God plan for Adam to turn (in rebellion) to his own way, yet He knew that in granting freedom of choice to man, the potential for disobedience was there.

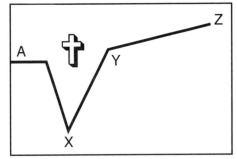

God knew (in His foreknowledge) what Adam would do. So the redemptive plan was incorporated from the beginning. Let no one assume that God was caught off-guard by Adam's wrong choice. We read about God's provision: the "Lamb slain from the foundation of the world." He had a rescue plan already in place. Through the death of His Son, Jesus, God would redeem man, and bring him back to the race-course so Adam could fulfill the original purpose of God.

Our great concern, as the title of this book reveals, is that often the religious world has left man in the small redemptive window, where he becomes mostly preoccupied with his own needs, and what God must do for him. Man thus ignores or has never recognized the larger window of God's purpose: what we do or become for Him.

In these past 40 years, many who have read our earlier books (where this theme is more fully considered) have expressed their amazement at the man-centered-ness of Christendom today. We do rejoice in having a small part in this awakening to God-centered-ness.

God's amazing grace must ever be magnified, but it must never be separated from His eternal purpose in Christ, as the wise Queen realized. Extending grace must lead to uncovering of man's deepest need, and finding and fulfilling the original purpose for his being.

We have pictured Adam standing at a gateway of choice: either to go God's way (A to Z) or to go his own way (A to X). From the beginning it was God's plan for Adam (and all mankind) to yield to God for fulfilling His purpose; thus Adam would be sustained by a divine life-union with God. It seems evident that the Source for that life-union was available to man in the garden, as represented by the Tree of Life. This would be the only Life-Source by which Adam could run the race and fulfill God's purpose. While Adam never did eat of that Tree of Life, no doubt he could have eaten, once the issue of committing himself to God for His purposes had been settled.

Here was the critical issue: Adam was either to live...
> (dependently) by the Tree of Life, or to live
> (independently) by eating of the tree of knowledge

FATHER, I hear You saying to me: "My child, You must lay aside all your own purposes if you would live for My Purpose." My heart responds:"Yes, I am willing that Your Purpose shall be my only purpose." Then I hear Your response: "My full supply of GRACE will always be available for THAT PURPOSE." Thank You, Father!

Consider This Critical Issue

We have purposed to select certain stories and place them in sequence to show how God is moving us from our beginning conceptions to the fuller understanding of all we possess in Christ Jesus. I like to call this spiritual progress our journey toward God's fullness. Because it helps me to visualize an idea, let me picture this three-wheel life-mobile to demonstrate the three essentials necessary for progress on our journey.

First, consider the two back wheels which drive our life-mobile. You may choose other drive-wheels, but for me HEARING and OBEYING are the two most clearly evident from God's Word. You will recall that immediately after God has taken His people, Israel, through the Red Sea—and they have started their journey to the land of promise—He exhorts: "If you listen carefully...and do what is right..." (and He repeats it again) "...if you pay attention...and keep..." Actually the more literal meaning of this phrase is: "...if listening, you will listen... and will do..." (Exod. 15:26)

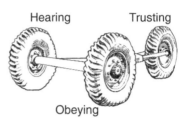

Once we recognize how significant our continual hearing and obeying really are, we will appreciate why this should be our day-by-day concern.

I am sure you have often marveled that our omnipotent God would devise this kind of plan (our hearing and doing) as His way of inviting us to participate with Him in fulfilling His Eternal Purpose.

Just how these two rear wheels of our life-mobile become the driving power will be more meaningful as we move along in these stories. However, there is another all important wheel!

As we have pictured, our life-mobile has a single front-wheel which is imperative in steering us toward God's End or Goal. To properly name and describe this all-important steering wheel will require a bit of explanation. For many years I would have said DISCERNMENT was the critical need for steering us toward God's goal, but now I have concluded differently. Though we may possess a confidence that we have heard God's voice and we have a confidence that we are obeying, there still remains our need for an "inner witness" that we are TRUSTING Him, and not leaning on our own understanding.

WHY IS THIS?: I believe God has very deliberately designed it that way. God does not want us depending on our own wisdom or understanding. In God's economy seeing is not believing, but TRUSTING begets seeing. We could summon the testimonies of scores of pilgrims who have honestly wrestled with the nature of this FRONT WHEEL. Each has discovered that TRUSTING is God's only way to reach His Goal:

Trust in the Lord with all thine heart, and lean not on your own understanding: in all your ways acknowledge him and he will make your paths straight (Prov. 3:5-6).

In the original Hebrew, "in all your ways acknowledge him" is more literally "in all your ways know him." This fundamental statement of how to relate to God implies more than mere reverence. Nodding in God's direction is not enough: you must know Him by living closely with Him, relating to Him personally in every aspect of your life.

Consider this testimony of a man who was caught by the devotion and sacrifice of Mother Theresa, and went to Calcutta to give himself in service for three months at 'the house of the dying'. He was seeking direction as to how best to spend the rest of his life. On the first morning there he met Mother Theresa. She asked, "And what can I do for you?" He simply asked that she pray for him.

"What do you want me to pray for?" she asked. In making his request he explained that he had travelled thousands of miles from the United States to serve there: "Pray that I have clarity."

She said firmly, "No, I will not do that." When he asked her why, she said, "Clarity is the last thing you are clinging to and must let go of." When this admirer commented that she (Mother Theresa) always seemed to have the clarity he longed for, she laughed and said, "I have never had clarity; what I have always had is TRUST. So I will pray that you TRUST God."

"We ourselves have known and put our TRUST in God's love toward ourselves" (1 John 4:16).

I hope you do not miss this critical issue: if we are granted clarity, or wisdom or discernment, then we can proceed without God (independently). This is His great controversy with each of us: we insist on knowing, but God simply responds:

TRUST Me, that I love you and know what is best.

I think this explanation offered by Brennan Manning sums it up: "Craving clarity, we attempt to eliminate the risk of TRUST-ING God. Fear of the unknown path stretching ahead of us destroys childlike TRUST in the Father's active goodness and unrestricted love...we often presume that TRUST will dispel the confusion, illuminate the darkness, vanquish the uncertainty, and redeem the times. But the crowd of witnesses in Hebrews 11 would testify that this is not the case. Our TRUSTING does not bring final clarity on this earth. It does not still the chaos or dull the pain or provide a crutch. When all else is unclear, the heart of TRUST says, as Jesus did on the cross, 'Into your hands I commit my spirit' " (Lk. 23:46 NIV).

So, **this front steering-wheel is TRUSTING.** It will become more evident that TRUSTING (which steers our life-mobile) is not produced by our searching, but it is (being) born through an intimate fellowship with Him. We do not run-into-His-presence-to-fellowship—as an act; rather we maintain a continuous abiding attitude and manner of life. This alone can steer us onward in FULFILLING God's Great Purpose. Finally we must ask: Am I whole-heartedly (yes, blindly) committing myself (as Jesus did) to the One who knows what is best? My Father is worthy of my TRUST or He isn't—that is the single issue!

When a spiritual mentor was asked to explain this more fully, he simply explained: "You've got enough insights to last you three hundred years. The most urgent need in your life is to TRUST what you have already received." And that is exactly where we begin and continue this journey. We are simply TRUSTING Him because there is nothing else we can do.

Purpose-Principle-Person

MANY YEARS AGO. . .
I was invited to a Bible church in Albuquerque. It was soon evident to me that the leadership was polarized and in a stalemate. God had been blessing this church and they had built a new sanctuary. Many new members had already been added, and it was the burden of certain leaders to help these new members become established and incorporated into their church life. To this end I was invited for a week of Bible teaching. There was, however, another group of leaders who wanted to emphasize evangelism and "fill the new sanctuary." When I recognized this leadership impasse, we met for prayer and fellowship. That afternoon I saw sitting on one side of the aisle all the "casters" who had a burning zeal for evangelism; on the other side I saw the "menders"—those who were burdened to teach and establish.

I asked the men to open their Bibles to Matt. 4:18-22. I explained when Jesus called Peter and Andrew, they were "casting their nets." And when He called James and John they were "mending their nets." In observing Jesus' disciples we see some were more gifted for evangelism (casters), while others were more gifted for establishing and training (menders). Each had their significant burden because of their gifting and calling. As each presented their case, I could recognize the leaders were not only sincere, but very articulate in showing why their burden was right.

Let me emphasize here that this kind of conflict often develops among those who love God. Whenever leaders of a church seek to chart plans for the coming year, there will be those who insist we must "wait on God" a bit longer for His direction. While others will insist "God is waiting on us," for He has already spoken, and we now need to become more active.

Anyone in leadership will have recognized that in approaching a problem we often have two differing mind-sets. There are those who tend...

...to be inclusive or to be exclusive,

...to be objective or to be subjective,

...to be rational (mental) or to be emotional-allow more feeling,

...to be practical (Corinthian) or to be spiritual (Ephesian),

...to be exact (literal) in interpretation, or to "spiritualize,"

I think we can recognize when we are primarily principle-centered we will inevitably reach a stalemate. This is simply the natural result of two mind-sets considering any principle. Someone has wisely described every principle as having a "right hand and a left hand aspect."

Instead of recognizing and properly dealing with both the "right and left hand" aspect of a principle, we are prone to go our separate ways. Too often the "casters" move across town to start their own fellowship and leave the "menders" behind. Thus we developed the Church of the Catchers, and the Church of the Menders.

Principles are foundational, and we must always give them a proper place, yet I am convinced we only invite more conflict as we remain principle-centered. (i.e. questioning whether the "casters" or the "menders" are right?)

For many years in my early ministry I was purpose-driven (achieving my goal was primary and since I was pre-occupied with the end result too often any means of achieving it was acceptable.) Then I saw the folly and became pre-occupied with understanding God's ways (the means by which He will fulfill His purpose.) What a thrill to emphasize God's ways (or principles). While I was not aware of it, I was becoming principle-centered. My pre-occupation was with principles. It was exciting to discover Biblical principles. But I was doomed for continual frustration, for every principle had its "right and left hand" aspect. Both were right, and I needed God's insight to understand which came first.

Then I entered a third pre-occupation, which meant turning from purposes and principles to become centered in trusting THE PERSON who has designed all the principles. This new pre-occupation has led me into a new fellowship and intimacy with a Person, the Lord, Himself.

In these stories we are seeking to demonstrate how God has above all, called us to move beyond principles to become Person-centered. It will become very evident to each reader that God has deliberately designed this universe:

>...to be PERSON-CENTERED.
>...to be PRINCIPLES-GOVERNED and
>...to be PURPOSE-FULFILLING

This is the proper way to reconcile two seemingly conflicting issues. It has seemed God always honors us with His answer when we will honestly bow before Him, acknowledge the conflict, and then seek to become wholly neutral-that is to lay aside every personal agenda. With the church-leadership mentioned above, it took some time of honest heart-searching, yet it did happen. When these men were willing to lay aside their own preference, their own agenda and with an honest heart, seek to know God's mind-they came to be wholly neutral. As they became occupied with Him, they asked, "God, what do You want?" The "menders" and the "casters" soon recognized that each was right, and that they needed to honor the gifting and burden of each other. They agreed both "casting" and "mending" needed to go on, yet there could be a special emphasis at certain times. The real issue was their willingness to be broken and to allow the Cross to work in them.

Those who are diligent in their study of principles have already discovered that every principle has its counter-part—it has what we call the right-hand and the left-hand aspect of that principle. And there is always a proper timing. The wise man, Solomon explains this in his wisdom book:

THERE IS A TIME TO VERY PURPOSE....
...a time to be born and a time to die,
...a time to plant and a time to uproot,
...a time to kill and a time to heal,
...a time to tear down and a time to build,
...a time to weep and a time to laugh,
...a time to embrace and a time to refrain,
...a time to keep and a time to throw away,
...a tune to be silent and a time to speak...(etc).

Only the Designer of Principles knows the right time, and He will unveil that time to us as we are occupied with Him.

FATHER, help us to see how You alone can keep us PER-SON-centered. Out of this dependence and intimacy You will show us which PRINCIPLES govern, and how and when they will fulfill Your PURPOSE. Help us to recognize that all three are imperative, but they have a divine sequence-one flows out of the other. And as we consider the following stories—establish one thing in our hearts: Every day the first important thing is for us to hear Your voice, and obey... then to TRUST you to work in YOUR OWN WAY.

My sheep hear my voice, and I know them, and they follow me." (John 10:27)

I Don't Believe There Is A God

WATCHMAN NEE EXPLAINS. . .
I was once holding evangelistic meetings in a college in South China. There I met an old friend, in fact an old school-fellow. He had been in America and was now in this college as Professor of Psychology. He claimed he had made up his mind about religion and now was in the habit of telling his students that he could explain all so-called conversions on purely psychological grounds.

Before the meetings began I went to call on him, and presented Christ to him. Out of politeness, he had to listen for a while, but finally, he smiled.

"It is no good preaching to me," he said. "I don't believe there is a God."

"Even if you do not believe in a God, just pray," I insisted—perhaps a little rashly. "You will discover something."

"Pray," he laughed, "when I don't even believe in a God! How could I," he exclaimed.

Then I said, "Though you cannot find a ladder up to God, it does not alter the fact that He has come down to find you. So you can just pray!"

He laughed again, but I still urged him to pray.

"I have a prayer that you can pray," I said. "Say this: 'O God, if there is no God, then my prayer is useless, and I have prayed in vain. But if there is a God, then somehow make me know it.'"

"But," he replied, "what has this hypothetical God got to do with Jesus Christ? Where does Christianity come in?"

I told him just to add a sentence to his prayer, asking God to show him this also. I explained that I was not asking him to admit there was a God. I was not asking him to admit anything. There was but one thing and one thing only that I asked of him—he must be honest. His heart must be in his prayer. It must not just be an empty repeating of words. I was not sure that I had accomplished anything. But when I went away I left with him a Bible.

The next day, at the end of the first meeting of my campaign, I asked any who had been saved to stand up, and the first one to do so was this professor. I went up to him afterwards.

"Has anything happened?"

"Much!" he replied. "Now I'm saved!"

"How did it happen?" I asked

"After you left yesterday, I picked up the Bible and opened it to John's Gospel. My eye caught the words, *'The day after... the next day... the day after.'* I thought to myself, this writer knows what he is talking about. He saw it all. It is like a diary.

"After that, I thought about what you had said to me. I tried to see if there was a catch in it, or if you were beguiling me in any way. I went over it, point by point, and I could see no flaw in it. It all seemed perfectly sound. Why should I not pray as you suggested?

"But suddenly the thought came to me: What if there is in fact a God? Where do I stand then? Having told my students that there is nothing in religion at all, and that psychology accounts for everything, am I willing to admit to them that I have been wrong all this time? I weighed this carefully. Nevertheless, I felt I had to be honest about it. For if after all, there really was a God, I would be a fool not to believe in Him!

"So I knelt down and prayed...And as I prayed, I just knew there was a God. How I knew, I cannot explain, but I just knew it! Then I remembered the Gospel of John that I had read, and how it seemed to be written by an eyewitness, and I knew that if that was so, then Jesus was the Son of God—and I became saved!" (WN)

> God will always honor:
> ....a hunger for reality,
> ....a heart honesty,
> ....a humility to face the truth

What confidence this brings, to know that God has spoken and continues to speak through His Word. Hearing God's voice is not difficult where this heart-hunger, heart-honesty and heart-humility are present. I always remember that God has been there first, before I arrived to present the Gospel. He has been preparing soil and I must realize the seeking Savior is ready to act in mercy and grace.

FATHER, my heart responds with a new expectancy. What You did for this professor, You will do for any heart that chooses to hear from Your Word, and then to obey with humility. This is my choice today, I will TRUST You.

Let us therefore come boldly unto the throne of grace, that we may obtain mercy, And find grace to help in time of need. (Heb. 4:16)

The Bible Can Do More

JOHN MACARTHUR WRITES

Not long ago a man I had never met before walked into my office. "I need help," he said. "I feel strange coming to you, because I'm not even a Christian. I'm Jewish! Until a few weeks ago, I had never even been in a church. But I need help from someone, so I decided to talk to you."

I assured him I would do my best to help him. I asked him to sit down and explain what was troubling him. The conversation went something like this:

"I've been divorced twice," he said, "and now I'm living with a woman who is my lover. I don't even like her, but I haven't got the courage to leave her and go back to my second wife.

"I'm a medical doctor," he continued. "Worse, I'm an abortionist! I kill babies for a living. Last year in my clinic we did nine million dollars' worth of abortions. I not only do abortions; I do abortions for any reason. And if a woman doesn't have a reason, I give her a reason.

"Six weeks ago I came to Grace Community Church on a Sunday morning, and I've been coming every week since. Last week you preached a message called, 'Delivered to Satan.' If there was ever anyone on earth who was delivered to Satan, it's me. I know I'm doomed to hell because of what I've done. I'm absolutely miserable and unhappy. I'm continually seeing a psychoanalyst, and I'm not getting any help at all. I can't stand the guilt of all this. I don't know what to do about it. Can you help me?"

"No," I said to him, "I can't help you."

He looked at me, startled. Sheer desperation was evident on his face. I let it sink in.

"But," I then said, "I know Someone who can help you—Jesus Christ."

"But I don't know who He is," he said sadly. "I've been taught all my life not to believe in Him."

"Would you," I said, "like to know who Jesus Christ is?"

"Yes, I would if He can help me," he answered.

"Here's what I want you to do."

I reached over and took a Bible off my desk and opened it to the Gospel of John.

"I want you to take this book home," I instructed, "and read this part called the Gospel of John. I want you to keep reading until you know who Jesus Christ is. Then call me again." Later that week I was recounting the incident for the pastor of another church.

"Is that all you gave him?" he asked. Just the Gospel of John? Why didn't you give him some helps, some tapes, some questions to answer—something? Just the Bible?"

"Don't worry," I replied. "The Bible is like a lion. You don't need to defend it. Just open the door, and let it out. It'll take care of itself. If his heart is open at all, the Bible can do more to reach him than I could do with reams of other study material. What could I possibly give him that's more powerful than Scripture itself?"

Next Friday, I received a telephone call. The doctor wanted to see me again. We made an appointment. He showed up precisely on time, came into the office, walked past me as if I weren't there, sat on the couch, and dropped the Bible beside him.

"I know who He is," he declared.

"You do?"

"Yes, I do," he answered.

"Who is He?"

"I'll tell you one thing—He's not just a man."

"Really?" I questioned. "Who is He?"

"He's God!" He said with finality.

"You, a Jew, are telling me that Jesus Christ is God?" I asked, "How do you know that?"

"It's clear. It's right there in the Gospel of John," he said.

"What," I asked, "convinced you?"

"Look at the words He said, and look at the things He did! No one could say and do those things unless He was God," he related, echoing the Apostle John's thesis perfectly.

I nodded enthusiastically.

He continued, "Do you know what else He did? He rose from the dead! They buried Him, and three days later, He came back from the dead! That proves He is God, doesn't it? God Himself came into this world"—he was on a roll.

"Do you know why He came?" I asked him.

"Yes. He came to do die for my sin."

"How do you know that?" I questioned.

"Because I liked John so well, I read Romans. And as soon as I clean up my life, I'm going to become a Christian."

"That's the wrong approach," I responded. "Receive Him as your Lord and Savior now, and let *Him* clean up your life."

I then asked the man, "What would such a decision mean to your career?"

"Well," he said, "I spent this afternoon writing my resignation letter to the abortion clinic. When I get out of here, I'm going to call my second wife and bring her to church with me." And this he did!

Why would anyone question Scripture's power to reach such a person? The fact is, nothing I could have ever said to that man would have been more effective than the Spirit-inspired truth of the Bible itself in convicting him of his sin and illuminating his need for Christ. (JMA)

Once again we see hunger-honesty-humility. Often God allows man to cooperate a bit in bringing someone to salvation. I especially like this story, for it seems to me that God is saying, "I'll do this one all by Myself, using My Word as My Spirit operates within him to bring this sinner to wholly trust Me."

If you question your ability to hear the Lord speak, consider how this Jewish abortion doctor understood what God was saying to him as he read the Gospel of John. It doesn't take any special training to hear from God's Word. As with the professor in the previous story, God honors our hunger for reality, our heart-honesty, and our humility to face any consequences His Lordship may require.

It becomes so evident: the more we read and heed His Word, the more we can expect God to speak to us. Consider this promise:

But God is rich in mercy...even when we were dead in sins, hath quickened us together with Christ, (by grace ye are saved;) And hath raised us up together and made us sit together in heavenly places in Christ Jesus: For by grace are ye saved through faith; and that not of yourselves: it is the gift of God. (Eph. 2:4-8)

FATHER, when I see how Your saving grace opened the eyes of this professor and this doctor, I know You not only awaken, but You quicken (make alive) those who have been dead in sins— those who have been following the course of this world. Help someone who is now reading this story to claim this divine quickening work of the Holy Spirit—and then to heed whatever You are asking them to do.

Jane's Reward

WHILE TRAVELING. . .
through the country-side holding gospel meetings, a preacher stopped at a restaurant to get his dinner. A most pleasant girl, about fifteen years of age, waited on him as he sat at the table. Now, it was the custom of this preacher whenever he met strangers to point out to them the way to heaven or to tell them something from God's Word that would help them.

This day before leaving the restaurant he asked the young waitress, "What is your name, my friend?"

"Jane, sir."

"Well, Jane, do you ever pray?"

"Oh, no sir," was her quick reply. "I've no time for anything like that. Why, I hardly have time to eat."

"Well, Jane, I want to make a bargain with you. I expect to be back here in about two months. I'll teach you a little prayer of only three words, which I want you to say every morning. It needn't take any time; for you can say it, if you like, while you are getting dressed. And when I come back, if you tell me you have said it every day, I'll give you this reward." He held up a bill which could be hers.

"I'll do it," said Jane, "I'll do it," with great resolve.

"Well, be sure and keep your promise."

"Yes, you may depend on that, for I always keep my promise," said Jane. "And now tell me what the prayer is."

"This is it," said the minister. "LORD, SAVE ME."

Then he shook hands with Jane, and said good-bye.

After two months he returned to the town and went into that restaurant for his dinner. Jane was not there, and another girl waited on him in her place. After eating, he spoke to the man who owned the place, and asked where Jane was.

"Oh, she took to going to meetings, and left here, and now she's living at the pastor's home down the road."

When he went to the pastor's home, he knocked at the door, and who should open it but Jane herself. As soon as she saw the minister, she reached out her hands and said, "You dear man! I'm so glad to see you again, and I want to thank you for teaching me that prayer. But I don't want your reward, because I've gotten enough."

"Well, let me know what you've got. Come, tell me more!"

"You see, sir, after you went away, I began to say that prayer every morning. At first I said it carelessly while I was getting dressed without thinking anything about it. But, one morning after I had said it, these two questions came into my mind: What did that gentleman want me to say this prayer for? What does 'save' mean? I thought the Bible would tell me something about it, so I borrowed one, and read in it a little every morning.

Pretty soon, I read one verse, which said: *'The Son of man is come to seek and to save that which was lost,'* and another verse said, *'Christ Jesus came into the world to save sinners.'* Then I saw that I was a lost sinner. This frightened me. I began to pray in earnest. I asked Jesus to pardon my sins, to save me and teach me how to love and serve Him. He heard my prayer. He has done all this for me, and more. Now I'm just as happy as the day is long. And I thank you for teaching me that prayer—but I won't take your money."

That was a most happy experience for Jane. One that she will never cease to thank the Lord for through time and eternity.

In previous stories we have considered how...

...Millie received the amazing phone number; how

...the young banker found his lost keys; how

...the professor discovered God in reading John, how

...the Jewish abortion doctor discovered who Jesus is.

Each in a very different way came to accept Jesus as His Lord and trust His death as payment for their sin-debt. This is amazing grace!

Perhaps you the reader, have never really trusted Christ as your Savior and entered into a living relationship with Him? You may be hearing His voice even now, *"Come unto me all ye that labor and are heavy laden and I will give you rest."* You do need rest! Right now, you could pray this same prayer: LORD, SAVE ME!

It is also possible that someone even now is praying for you and asking God that you will make this choice. If someone has given this book to you, they are asking for God's best in your life. (Whatever that may be). There are many who are convinced that God will honor their planting (a book), then watering by prayer, and they are fully expecting God to give increase (win someone to Himself.)

FATHER, I am thankful it is so simple to trust You. As Jane did, I pray many others will pray that simple prayer. Amen!

The Tract Returns

MANY OF THE WEALTHY ARISTOCRATS. . . who ruled England from London in the nineteenth century were known for living lives of empty pleasure. Some praying Christians decided they would make a special effort to reach this upper class.

It was unlikely that they would respond to an invitation to a gospel meeting and attend with commoners. So this concerned group agreed upon another way—mail gospel tracts to them.

Inside his elegant estate, a distinguished gentleman settled down at his desk to open his morning mail. Included was a plain white envelope, simply addressed. George sliced it open and curiously pulled out the small leaflet.

His eyes scanned the first few lines. He immediately recognized it as "religious propaganda."Who dared send him such a thing? To suggest that he was not going to heaven! Did they know who he was? He was doing fine by himself!

Suddenly, George's scowl changed to a smirk. He and his friend, Edward, were always playing practical jokes on one another. This would be perfect. Selecting another envelope, he wrote the address with as simple handwriting as he could. Yes, he mused to himself, this would really get to Edward. Then he proceeded to send it along the way.

A few days later, in another estate, a few miles away, Edward opened the envelope, skimmed the first few lines, and responded just as his friend surmised he would. He was about to toss the paper into the fire. Suddenly his hand drew back. Indeed it was God's appointed moment. If someone had taken the time to send this to him, the least he could do was read it. As he read, it was like penetrating light that exposed his own sinfulness and God's great love for sending His Son to die for him. He hadn't heard this since he was a boy. (Those who planted were watering the tract.)

Before the sun set that day, Edward entered into a personal relationship with the Lord and trusted Him as his Savior.

His immediate impulse was to share the news. Getting out another envelope, he addressed it to his old friend, George. He prayed that God would bless the tract again.

You can imagine George's amazement! This was a little unnerving. He thought Edward would burn the tract, but here it was again. George looked at the little messenger for a moment, then slowly began to read. He, too, was convicted of his need of a Savior and trusted the finished work of Christ for himself that day.

Some time later when the two met, they put together the story of the tract that had been the means of their salvation. They not only laughed at the providential working of God, but they began to work together faithfully to bring others the good news.

Why was this tract successful? You will observe that some praying Christians had a burden to send out these tracts. They were not only planting (tracts) but were diligent in watering (praying) over the tracts that the seed would fall into good soil.

There is a great emphasis abroad today on planting seed and expecting the harvest. I always rejoice! But I could wish there was an equal burden to water the seed being planted. God has indeed promised:

> *"Those who sow in tears shall reap in joy.*
> *He who continually goes forth weeping,*
> *Bearing seed for sowing, shall doubtless*
> *Come again with rejoicing, bringing*
> *His sheaves with him."* (Ps. 126:5-6)

My Lord, I hear You asking when I last wept over some seed I had planted. I realize that watering is more than casual praying! I hear You saying: It is tearful waiting upon Me to accomplish the desire for which You pray. Yes Lord, I cannot manufacture tears, but I can ask You to give me Your own burden for the lost. Help me to remember someone who needs this book—to whom I might send and water it with much prayer.

Casting Down Reasonings

IT WAS DURING A WEEK
of ministry in a church/school that I came to recognize the difference between having a reason(ing) and a right. Let me explain
how this happened:

The Headmaster of the school summoned one of the senior
boys into the office because he had become resentful and argu-
mentative. Once helpful and courteous and ambitious, now suddenly his attitude had drastically changed.

When the senior boy arrived in the office, at first he refused to
explain his behavior. Then he burst forth, "You'd be angry too
if you had a father like mine!" He told us that his father boarded
special horses for wealthy people. "A month ago my father shot
my pet pigeons because they were messing up the hay in the barn
loft. These were choice pigeons, and my father could have given
me time to move them. Then, last week my father shot my dog
when it got sick and vomited in the aisle of the barn. "You see," he
exploded, "I've got a right to be angry with a father who is so
inconsiderate."

Of course our sympathy reached out to him, for it seemed
obvious he had been treated unfairly–if his story was correct.
Perhaps the father needed to be called in for counsel.

Up to this point I had only listened to the conversation. Now I
had an urge to explain to him the difference that I saw between
having a reason(ing) and having a right.

I drew a diagram of a tree planted by the river. I explained
that all of us who are God's children have a privileged position of
being planted by the Lord near that river. Then I drew roots that
extended down to the river of grace and explained that God had
made available to all of us the rich supply of His grace—if we
would respond correctly.

I explained that grace is not only a favored position (Rom. 5:1)
wherein we stand as a tree by the river, but we need a fuller understanding that God in grace is quick to supply the desire and ability
to respond to every unfair situation. Because of this enabling grace
which he could now receive, he had no "right" to be angry.

Looking directly into his eyes I explained, "There is one thing
you need to do. What do you think that is? Do you see your roots?

What will cause your roots to go down to take from the river of grace?" I waited silently for his reply. "We had agreed that what his father had done did not seem fair. It surely was not proper for a Christian father. But now he had his own personal problem with God. He must recognize this difference between hiding behind his reason(ing) and his right to draw grace from the river.

His reasoning that his father was wrong, and that he was justified in being angry with him was not acceptable before God. Why? Because God had provided a supply of grace for everyone who is treated unfairly! So he had no right to be angry—if God had made a provision for such a time. He had the right (privilege) to send his roots down into the river of grace and God would give him the desire and ability to forgive his father. But he needed to do one thing!

I opened my Bible to read Paul's words: "...casting down imaginations (or reasoning) and every high thing that exalts itself against the knowledge of God..." (2 Cor. 10:5). I explained: "You see you are having an argument with God (your reasoning) why you have a right to be disappointed with Him and your father. But you have no right–since God has made ample provision to give you the desire and ability to forgive your father. You have no right to be angry."

I could see he was breaking as tears fell from his eyes. I drew another tree by the river, and explained he could become like that tree whose roots curled up instead of down. He could choose to have a root-life that is receiving grace, or one that is resisting God's offer of grace.

"I choose this tree." He pointed to the second tree with roots down.

"Good," I continued. "Both Peter and James explain the one thing necessary for you to receive God's grace: Will you humble yourself!

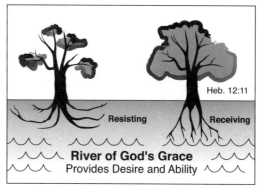

Immediately he knelt by his chair and poured out his heart, asking God to forgive him, and also asking God to give him this desire and ability to forgive his father. It was just a few minutes and he arose with a new countenance. He explained: "God has forgiven me, and I have forgiven my father. I will go home immediately and explain to him where I have been wrong."

God's Word is very clear:

"....*God resists the proud, but gives grace to the humble...*" (James 4:6) *again,*
"....*God resists the proud, and gives grace to the humble...*" (I Pet. 5:5).

FATHER, help me to recognize my reasonings, and cast them down. I see that Your enabling grace is always available for every bitter circumstance. If I humble myself... I will not need to be humbled.

The Bus Missed Her

A MOTHER WRITES
how her child's school bus driver had become a bitter Christian.
Once the father of eleven children, now only nine sat around his
family table. All were shocked when a drunken driver plowed
through his property and took the life of a son and a daughter.
Though he knew better, he blamed God for the accident and
grew hard and cold in his bitter anguish. In himself he could find
no forgiveness toward the man who had broken his family circle.
(He had no experience of receiving from God's river of grace.)

Then came a turn of events. One day when school was dismissed the teacher assigned to watch the children board the
school bus was late. As our daughter, Michelynne, passed in front
of the bus, she dropped some papers. In bending over to pick
them up, the bus driver did not see her. The moving bus knocked
Michelynne to the ground, smashed her lunch pail, but the wheels
passed on either side of her body. It was amazing! She received
only a cut on the top of her head. We were most grateful to God
that her life had been spared.

Early the next morning the bus driver came to see us. He
talked about his son's and daughter's accident which had happened eleven months earlier, and how he had not been able to forgive the driver. Now he had understanding! He wondered if we
could forgive him for what he had done? We explained that we
had already forgiven him.

Immediately his whole family started attending church; the
bus driver rededicated his life to the Lord and his wife received
the Lord Jesus. Over the next months other members of his family
trusted Christ as Lord and Savior.

Listen to this mothers testimony of how she responded to the
supply of God's grace: "A few days before this accident occurred
someone had loaned me a book, POWER IN PRAISE. That book
made a change in my life. I soon had opportunity to use what I
had learned. That day the kindergarten teacher and the school
nurse brought Michelynne to our home from the accident, as they
were telling me what had happened to my daughter, I thanked...
and praised the Lord for His mercy. Ordinarily I would have 'fallen
apart.' "

Someone has said, "Never face any trouble without first thanking God for it. Then the trouble is no longer a mere trouble, it is an opportunity for God to give victory through the trouble."

Consider Paul's words: *"Rejoice at all times..."* (1 Thess. 5:16)

The secret of rejoicing at all times is the next:

"Never give up prayer" (17). And the outcome is:

"In everything give thanks" (18).

Once you have moved beyond the mere act of prayer to the attitude of prayer, then thanksgiving becomes a way of life and you will daily maintain an ability to forgive.

Having reached this point in our journey, we need to be convinced that nothing hinders prayer so much as holding little resentments or nurturing an unforgiving spirit.

I repeat, we must be convinced—convinced that we will reap consequences and that we must also stop justifying. Don't get hung up on your attempt to justify the resentment by calling it "righteous indignation." Yes, there is such a thing as righteous indignation. Jesus had it when He *"looked around about on them with anger, being grievous for the hardness of their hearts."* (Mark 3:5)

But Jesus' anger was at what was happening to someone else, and not personal pique at what was happening to Him. Jesus was "being grieved"—at what was happening to another. When our anger has a grief in it (at what is happening to someone else), and not a gripe because of what is happening to us, then the anger is right and righteous." Remember, even though some anger is righteous, don't keep it (overnight) i.e. too long within your heart. It will surely fester.

This is why Paul warns: *"Be angry and sin not. Let not the sun go down upon your wrath"* (Eph.4:26). So, there is an anger that can be held without sin. But if you are to be angry and sin not, then you must be angry only at sin, and it must not be kept overnight. For even a righteous indignation can eat away the love side of your life and leave you righteously cantankerous—an unlovely person.

FATHER I want my life to demonstrate grace-full reactions in all life's circumstances. I remember again, that it is only as I cast down all "reasonings" and humble myself under Your hand that I can expect to receive the desire and power to forgive. While I am not inwardly searching for something now, I do choose to forgive whatever You bring to my remembrance. Yes, I will send my roots down to take from the river of Your grace and maintain a forgiving attitude.

Expectations

ELIZABETH ELLIOT TELLS OF. . .
a couple who had been married only a week or two when the wife went out shopping. The husband wondered what he might do for her while she was gone that would please and surprise her and show her how much he loved her. A brilliant plan came to mind. He got down on hands and knees and scrubbed the kitchen floor. It was a demeaning task in his opinion, and he felt exceedingly humble while performing it. How amazed Ann would be! He waited in eager anticipation of her return, thinking how blessed it is to give.

She drove in the driveway, breezed into the kitchen, set the grocery bags on the counter, and glanced at the floor.

"Oh—the floor's clean. Thank you, honey!" was all she said and went about putting things away.

The man told me he went into a three-day funk. He was hurt; he was insulted; he was not properly appreciated; and the blessing of giving drained out in an instant because he had not received the kind of thanks he had expected. His expectations were shattered!

Ann had no idea what the trouble was. What she did not know was that her husband had never heard of a husband's doing such a thing as scrubbing a floor for his wife, especially voluntarily, having thought of it all by himself. What he did not know was that in his wife's family no woman ever did the job. Her father considered it a man's job and did it as a matter of course.

That young husband took the lesson to heart. He now believes that it would be wise for every Christian to post as his motto the lesson Jesus taught; "We are servants and deserve no credit; we have only done our duty." Learning to dwell together takes much patience.

Of course this relationship (husband and wife) was intact, but there was a shadow over their fellowship until he recognized this simple misunderstanding. John and Ann each had their expectations! (E.E.)

So, each of us has had our time of disappointment, when our expectations were not fulfilled. King David understood this and wrote:

My soul, wait silently for God alone, for my expectation is from Him.

FATHER, when I realize how sufficient You are, I will not look to others for fulfillment. Today I hear Your reminder: "Wait silently for (Me) God alone." And my heart responds, Yes! I will TRUST!

Only Grace Could Do This

IN A LARGE WEALTHY CITY-CHURCH. . . it was the custom to invite their three mission churches on the first Sunday of each new year to a joint communion service. In those missions were some outstanding examples of conversion: thieves, burglars, outcasts—all knelt side by side in taking the communion.

On one such occasion, the pastor saw a converted burglar kneel beside a judge of the Supreme Court —the very judge who had sentenced him to jail where he had served seven years.

When he was released, the burglar had an amazing testimony of conversion and became a devoted worker. Neither seemed to recognize the other even though they knelt beside each other.

After the service, the judge was walking home with the pastor. He asked him, "Did you notice who was kneeling beside me at the altar during the Lord's Table this morning?"

"Yes, I did not know that you noticed him."

Presently the judge exclaimed, "What a miracle of grace!"

"Yes, a marvelous miracle of grace," replied the pastor. "But to whom do you refer?" queried the judge. "So-and-so," said the pastor, mentioning the name of the burglar.

"I was not referring to him," said the judge. "I was thinking of myself." "You were thinking of yourself?" "Yes, it did not cost that burglar much to get converted when he came out of jail. He had nothing but a history of crime behind him, and when he saw Jesus as his Savior, he knew there was salvation and hope for him.

"But look at me! I was taught from earliest infancy to live as a gentleman; that my word was to be my bond; that I was to say my prayers, go to church, take communion, and so on. I went through Oxford, took my degrees, was called to the bar, and eventually became a judge. Pastor, nothing but the grace of God could have caused me to admit that I was a sinner on a level with that burglar! Do you not agree it was much harder for me to humble myself than it was for that burglar?"

FATHER, let us never forget, that at the cross each of us is reduced to the lowest place—we become as "zeros", whether from high or low estate. You have heard the desire of the humble; You will prepare their heart; You will cause Your ear to hear.

Surely, to the humble... You give more... and more... and more grace!

"For This I Have Jesus"

MANY YEARS AGO. . .
in a small church in Ireland, a message was given about Jesus' words, *"Abide in me, and I in you."* The minister said it means to simply say in every circumstance, *"For This I Have Jesus, and Jesus will say, 'For This You Have Me.'"*

While he was speaking, a telegram was delivered to Helen, the young pianist.

"Mother very ill," she read to herself, "take first train home."

At the conclusion of the message, Helen shared the telegram with us. "I have never traveled alone," she added, "but, *'For This I Have Jesus.'* I must take a midnight train, but *'For This I Have Jesus.'* I must cross the channel and make connections on the other side, but *'For This I Have Jesus.'* Then I take a long train trip to the south of England, but *'For This,'* and all the suspense along the way, *'I Have Jesus.'"*

As she spoke these words, we saw the Light of Heaven upon Helen's face.

Several weeks later, a letter came from her which was a song of praise. She explained: "As I traveled that long sorrowful journey, I continued to say, *'For This I Have Jesus,'* and He answered, *'For This You Have Me.'*

"As I reached home my sister fell sobbing on my shoulder. 'Oh, if you had come ten minutes sooner,' she said, 'you would have seen Mother–who longed to see you.'

"Instantly, I looked up and said, *'For This I Have Jesus.'*

"And He came between me and my sorrow. Vain regrets that I might have for coming so late had no power over me. We had never had a death or a funeral in our family. They all depended on me for every decision. Acknowledging my ignorance, I said softly, *'For This I Have Jesus.'* Yes, He gave me His wisdom for every detail, and also His perfect peace to handle all legal matters that needed attention. Ever since, my life has become joyous and victorious, because in every circumstance I continue to say, *'For This I Have Jesus.'"*

Consider another amazing testimony of grace. When Jed Jackson, popular T.V. sportscaster in Colorado Springs, discovered he was losing his battle with cancer, thousands of e-mails, letters, and cards poured into his hospital room expressing love and encouragement.

To express his appreciation, Jed wrote this short statement that was printed on the front page of the newspaper the day after his death. To most of his readers, Jed had earned the right to speak:

"It has been my sincere privilege to serve this wonderful community, which has given me so much in return. The Lord has blessed my life in every possible way. He has given me my wife of 19 years, my three splendid children, and more friends than a man should be allowed to have. I am overwhelmed by the kind regards so many of you have sent. Truly my cup runs over. Never forget that, with Jesus, the best is yet to come."

We might wonder how Helen and Jeb could comfort others in their time of difficulty? Paul tells us that we learn *"to comfort others with the comfort we have received."* We are to become a fountain that overflows with comforting words. *"Let your speech always be with grace, seasoned with salt, that you may know how to answer each one"* (Col. 4:6)

FATHER, I want to enjoy this same abiding-life, (living with my roots in your river of grace)—that when difficult times come— I will have my continual supply in You, and also enough for others. I desire to demonstrate—so others will be convinced: You are wholly sufficient for every trial. Amen!

Hearing God For Life

PETER LORD WRITES. . .
If we open our hearts and minds to the Lord's guidance in all facets of our lives, we will discover that He is interested in everything about us. We can enter into fellowship with Him, knowing that He cares about each of the day-to-day happenings that come our way. Learning that God communicates His continual concern for the ordinary things we care about is sometimes surprising, as it was to me in the following examples:

The Toy Calculator

In the summer of 1985, Johnnie and I made a tour of the Far East to speak to missionaries there. In Singapore, I purchased a toy—a $2.50 calculator no bigger than a credit card. Its size and technology so fascinated me that I indulged in the luxury of an unnecessary purchase.

On the way home to Florida we stopped at Woodland Park, Colorado, to visit our son and his family. As a souvenir of the trip, I gave Richard the $2.50 calculator and began to show him how it worked. Except it didn't! All I got were sporadic numbers. My toy was broken–so I assumed!

I was disgusted. I had wasted money and had violated a concept I sought to live by—"The bitterness of poor quality lingers long after the sweetness of cheap price has been forgotten."

"Johnnie," I said to my wife, "don't ever let me buy a cheap thing like that again!" Late that night I was still awake, trying to adjust to the ten-hour time change.

"Peter," the Lord Jesus said while I was in fellowship with Him, "there's nothing wrong with your calculator. It's just the altitude here. Take it back to Florida, and it will work properly."

Well, I did bring it back home with me, and it's functioning as well as new. I am learning to appreciate His speaking to me.

The Blocked Toilet

Our son Richard has five sons. One thing is inevitable—almost as certain as the sunrise. If you have five small children, one of them will flush something large down a toilet.

Sure enough, one of the boys tried to flush away a wedge-shaped block. It was stuck in the toilet trap. Richard tried and tried to get it out. Finally, thoroughly frustrated, he called a plumber. This paid professional worked at the problem with his tools for some time. "The only way to get that out," he said, "is with a sledge hammer."

"You mean I'll have to replace the toilet?" asked Richard.

"Yup," answered the plumber.

It was then that I arrived on the scene. Richard could not afford a new toilet and asked me to look at it. I worked fruitlessly a long time. At last, I too gave up. Finally, I asked the Lord for wisdom.

He told me exactly what to do. In ten minutes the block was out and the toilet was working again.

"Wait!" I can hear you say. "Our Lord is not interested in such mundane things as a $2.50 calculator and a jammed toilet!"

That's exactly what I used to think, until He reminded me, *"My eye is on the sparrow"*—and it's on you, too. "I am a father who cares about every aspect of my children's lives. I enjoy fixing things for you as you enjoy fixing things for your children."

Don't misunderstand me, God doesn't always say "Yes." He doesn't always give us an easy way out. I just want to point out that He cares, and He always answers in some way. But we must learn to listen.

The Seat Belt

One Saturday in January 1986, I was headed to another town to make a ministry visit. As I left the house, the Lord suddenly reminded me, 'Fasten your safety belt.' This was before the days when a mandatory seat-belt law was in effect in Florida, and in those days I sometimes was careless about buckling up on short trips.

My inner response was, "Oh, nothing is going to happen."

"That's what everybody always thinks!" God reminded me.

The message was clear, so I obeyed and fastened my seat belt.

Less than ten minutes later, I was driving along at fifty-five miles an hour on an open two-lane highway. Suddenly a car pulled out from a side road without stopping, zooming right into my path. There was no place to swerve safely, and I barely had time to hit the brakes.

A collision was unavoidable under the circumstances. Both cars were badly smashed. But I came out of it without even a bruise—thanks to the Lord's watchful care. This was another evidence that the Father cares and communicates at all times and in all things. Evidence of our need for an active, vital fellowship with the Lord.

The Lost Diamond

While we were visiting our daughter in Texas, the diamond in my wife's engagement ring dropped out of its setting. It was only a small diamond—all I had been able to afford as a college student. But its sentimental value to both of us was great.

We asked the Lord to help us find it. And He did! It was a miracle, because it had fallen into the carpet pile. God guided our search, and we found the stone. Then my wife, Johnnie, carefully put the diamond in a secure place in our suitcase. For one of the first things we wanted to do when we got home was to have it reset.

When Johnnie unpacked at home and looked for the diamond, it wasn't where she had put it. She searched in every part of the suitcase, but the diamond was gone. We even called Texas and asked our daughter to look for it. Of course, we prayed about it.

This time, there was no answer and no diamond. In due time, we gave up, and accepted the loss as permanent. The diamond was forgotten, crowded from my mind by the urgency of my other responsibilities.

Some time later one morning, as I was in fellowship with the Lord Jesus, He said to me, "Peter, the diamond is in your bedroom at home—in the dresser."

And that's exactly where it was! The tiny stone had gotten hidden in some seldom-used items in that suitcase and ended up in the dresser drawer. Now the diamond is again where it ought to be—on my wife's ring finger. Some of the lessons I learned are:

God is interested in the smallest details of your life. 'Toy' calculators, jammed toilets, and lost diamonds are equally significant, even as *"the very hairs of your head are all numbered"* (Matt. 10:30, NIV).

God's answers are often delayed.

Many things happen while we are in fellowship with the Lord, which do not happen when we are pressing Him for answers. We must guard against our human tendency to use God and only go to Him when we want something from Him. (P.L.)

FATHER. I see that You delight to direct those who enjoy a fellowship with You that is for Your own pleasure and not for our "getting something."

God Supplied Both

HERBERT CROUCH OF LONDON EXPLAINS. . . On a Saturday a few years ago I could not fix upon either a text or a subject for my sermon the next morning. While at tea a bit later, a verse from Psalm 144 came forcibly to my mind and opened up to me most wonderfully. I hastened to my study and made notes, lest the thoughts given to me should escape.

The next morning after I had preached, a lady approached me and as she offered her hand said, "I am a stranger, having only been in this city three days. Yesterday I was in great anguish and went to my room. As I opened my Bible my eyes fell upon this very verse from which you took your text this morning. I knelt and read the entire Psalm, and when I came to the last verse I pleaded with God regarding this terrible anxiety that was burdening my heart."

Then I asked Him, "Oh, Lord, if thou wilt permit me to hear a sermon in the morning from that last verse of this Psalm, I will believe that You will undertake for me. I hardly realized what I said, but now I know—how good our God is."

After more inquiry pastor Crouch made this discovery: "I found that my special leading for the sermon came at the very moment this lady was praying about her anxiety."

Pastor Crouch continues: Let me share the thoughts which led to that last verse of Psalm 144. While preaching I gave this description of a truly happy land where Jehovah is God—the One Who delights to be the Supplier of every need:

"Sons vigorous and tall as growing plants.
Daughters of graceful beauty like the pillars of a palace wall.
Barns full to the brim with crops of every kind.
Sheep by the thousands out in our fields.
Oxen loaded down with produce.
No enemy attacking the walls, but peace everywhere.
No crime in the streets.
Yes, happy are those whose God is Jehovah!" (Living Bible)

It is always a delight to hear of God's guidance to any searching heart. It is just one of many ways (we will consider more later) of God's special guidance.

In this present story I am quite aware we are considering a very "touchy" area of divine guidance. I say touchy because many of the cults or cultic practices have developed from following inward impulses. Yet everyone knows as he grows in any spiritual measure, that he must sooner or later see the importance of following the Holy Spirit's inward prompting. I know fire is dangerous, but it is also necessary and can be properly regulated in the stove. If we expect to hear His voice, we must learn to recognize the monitions of the Holy Spirit.

"It is hoped that this account will illustrate something of the Holy Spirit's prompting and guidance. However, it should not be imagined that all prayer in the Spirit is as dramatic as this or that only such obvious promptings are to be considered prayer in the Spirit." (H.C.)

Remember, God initiates by giving inward prompting—never contrary to His Word. But don't seek for them, and yet don't ignore God's attempt to lead you by them. For many years I have sought to follow this caution of J. I. Packer who writes:

"Our rational Creator guides His rational creation
by rational understanding and application of His written Word."

I wish every one of us could frame that for a motto on our wall. I not only agree, but would emphasize the importance of diligently searching and obeying God's written word. It is the only safe way of guidance. This is our unique privilege of expecting God to take a (Logos) word we may have known for years and to quicken it into a (Rhema) word for that moment, even as He did with Dr. Crouch.

FATHER, I know the initiative is with You, but the delightful expectation in me is that You desire to "...lead me in a straight path..." to "lead me in the way of righteousness..." and "lead me in paths that I have not known..." Amen!

Help In My Praying

EDITH MARSHALL EXPLAINS:
SEVERAL MONTHS after my husband, Peter, had accepted the pastorate and we had moved to the picturesque village of East Dennis on Cape Cod, I was invited to come and pick raspberries in the backyard of one of the wisest and dearest men I have ever known. He was the Rev. John Stanton, retired Presbyterian minister.

Carrying my berry-picking basket, I wandered up the crushed shell driveway beside a weathered-shingle, rambling house. He was sitting in the backyard, a huge Bible in his lap, his eyes closed, his lips moving. I knew he must be praying—except for the fact that every once in a while his eyes would open to focus on the Bible, only to be shut tight in a few seconds.

In a few moments he spotted me out of the corner of his eye, and beckoned me over with a warm welcome.

"I don't mean to interrupt, " I apologized.

"Oh," he chuckled, "I'm praying my way through Psalms. It's marvelous!"

As I looked puzzled, he explained that because so many of the Psalms are addressed to the Lord, they lend themselves to being incorporated into our own personal prayer-life and that he was simply personalizing them as his own prayer. His prayers were rich as a result–full of praise and thanksgiving. And since his supplications were prayed according to the will of God, he had the assurance his prayers would be answered. But not wanting to seem super-spiritual, he showed me to the berry patch and set me to work.

Since my prayer life seemed dull at the time, I determined to try Dr. John's approach. The very next morning with my Bible opened in front of me, I began praying out loud the passages that lent themselves to prayer. Some Psalms needed very little paraphrasing before they could be my own heart-felt prayer:

Create in me a clean heart, O God, and put a new and right spirit within me. Cast me not away from your presence, and take not your Holy Spirit from me. Restore to me the joy of thy salvation and uphold me with a willing spirit. (Ps. 51:10-12)

Other Psalms could become my own prayers simply by changing some words and making them personal:

Lord, you are my shepherd. When you're there I have no needs.

You make me still in the inner man and give me peace. You lift up, restore, and heal my soul. Please lead me in your paths of righteousness For your name's sake...(Psalm 23)

On my next visit to Dr. Stanton's, I shared with him my newfound enthusiasm for praying the Psalms. And I added that certain passages in the New Testament also pointed up my needs, such as:

Oh, Lord, let me live by the Spirit and walk by the Spirit. Free me from self-conceit. Let there be in me no provoking of another and no envy. (Gal. 5:25)

Or if there was something I didn't understand:
Lord, how can I work out my salvation with fear and trembling?

Is there something I must do, or something to repent of. Show me Lord. (Phil. 2:12)

Dr. John confirmed my experiences thus far, and then taught me about using the Scriptures to intercede for others: "Do the same things you've been doing in praying for yourself," he said. "But now put the other person's names in the Scripture passage wherever it's appropriate." I could do this in the following way:

Oh, Lord, you who have begun a good work in (Ellen)...bring it to completion (in her). (Phil. 1:6) Or,

Blessed be the Lord who daily bears (Ellen) up. God is (her) salvation (Ps.68:19-20).

I found that on nearly every page of the Bible there was a phrase or a sentence that I could turn into prayer for someone else. There were also Scriptures with promises I could claim for others:

Oh, Lord, as (Ellen) passes through the waters and rivers, be with her, that they not overflow (her). Keep her from being burned by fire. (Isa. 43:2)

As (Ellen) walks through this affliction, work in her a far more exceeding and eternal weight of glory. (2 Cor. 4:17)

What a wealth of resource and inspiration for prayer is available when we but open His Word. (E.M)

Most of us have tried some new technique for improving our quiet time with the Lord, and we have practiced it "for a while." Then someone explained another method for developing more intimacy or enthusiasm in our praying. And we tried that for a while, with some progress. Eventually we must come to realize it is not some new technique or method we need. Usually ours is not so much a head problem, as a heart problem. When our heart is focused on Him, when our heart is devotional, i.e. passionate toward Him, then can we turn any quiet time into meaningful reality. We will soon discover, as we are praying the Psalms a couple times a week—they will remain living and fresh encounters with Him. Really it is our heart-passion in praying that counts.

It is important that we emphasize again for those who are finding their devotional time difficult—there is no by-passing our need for:
...dedication—the discipline of staying-with prayer,
...discernment—seeing with the Spirit's anointing,
...devotion—a singleness of heart-passion for Him.

FATHER, I am so thankful that I have discovered this way of praying Your Word back to You. When my heart is truly seeking to know You, and my focus is free from distractions around me that would overwhelm me, then I can love You with a singleness. Even as Edith learned to identify with the Psalmist in his crying for help, in his times of thankfulness, in his times of praise and adoration, so let my devotional life increase until I look forward to being with You each morning

Excellent Grace

I WANT TO PASS ON. . . the classic story of a woman who kept a secret locked in her heart for fifty years. It still moves me today as when I read it many years ago.

"I was twenty and he was twenty-six. We had been married two years, and I hadn't dreamed he could be unfaithful. The awful truth was brought home to me when a young widow from a neighboring farm came to see me. She told me she was carrying my husband's child. My world collapsed. I wanted to die. I fought an urge to kill her. And him!

"I knew that wasn't the answer. I prayed for strength and guidance. And it came. I knew I had to forgive this man, and I did. I forgave her, too. I calmly told my husband what I had learned and the three of us worked out a solution together. What a frightened little creature she was!

"The baby was born in my home. Everyone thought I had given birth and that my neighbor was 'helping me.' Actually, it was the other way around. But the widow was spared humiliation— she already had three other children.

"And the little boy? He was raised as my own. He never knew the truth.

"Was this divine compensation for my own inability to bear a child? I do not know. I have never mentioned this incident to my husband. It has been a closed chapter in our lives for fifty years. But I've read the love and gratitude in his eyes a thousand times!"

God's abundant supply of grace is always available to the humble, and He will reward those who walk in wisdom:

"...an ornament of grace unto thy head, and chains about thy neck." (Pr. 1:9)
"...they shall be life unto thy soul, and grace to thy neck." (Pr. 3:22)
"...shall give to thine head an ornament of grace, and a crown of glory shall she deliver thee." (Pr. 4:9)

FATHER, it is wonderful to realize You are seeking those who will become demonstrators of Your grace. Your reward is not only enjoying more grace, it is wearing the ornament of grace and glory.

Not Why... But What...

RUTH PAXSON, missionary to China, tells about a woman who boarded a train with her in Finland. The first thing Miss Paxson noticed was her radiant face (evidence of an inner joy). But then she observed that the woman's right hand was missing, and in its place was a steel hook.

As they talked, Miss Paxson learned that she had been a missionary in India, had contracted a lung disease and had been sent home to die. Upon returning to Finland, she bought a farm.

One day, while she was working on the threshing machine, her right hand was cut off. Now, as the two talked on the train, she told Miss Paxson, "When my hand was cut off, I immediately looked up to my Lord and said, 'Lord, what do you want me to do now that my right hand is gone? What work? I'm not asking why? But what?'"

Undaunted by her limitation, God burdened her to turn her farm into a home for elderly Christians—thus bringing blessing to many in their closing years.

When seeming adversity like this strikes, how quickly the enemy comes in and whispers, "The Lord is against you! This could not be the goodness of the Lord! Surely this kind of life is not what the Lord promised you." If we are not careful, we will accept his accusation: "The Lord is a hard task master to serve; this life is not all it was represented to be; your God has deceived you!" (R.P.)

We do not deny that adversity, trials and suffering come to believers as well as to others in the world, but they do not mean the Lord is against us. We need to understand Oswald Chamber's warning:

"The root of all evil is the suspicion that God is not good."

Please remember, God did not send it, but He will use it, as nothing else, to help you know Him. Therefore, we do not ask why, but simply what could be more important than knowing Him.

"...let him that glorieth, glory in this, that he understandeth and knoweth me; that I am the Lord which exercise lovingkindness, judgment and righteousness in the earth; for in these things I delight..." (Jer. 9:24)

FATHER, My heart responds: what a faithful God we serve—totally worthy of our trust!

The Supreme Test

WHILE VISITING WITH ONE. . . of God's choice servants I happened to notice the notations along the margin of many pages in his Bible. I was curious, so I said, "Some folk underline verses that are very special to them, but I see you have placed dates by certain verses. "Yes," he explained, "through the years I have experienced many opportunities to prove the Word.

"What God has recorded in His book is completely trustworthy, yet I have had the privilege personally of proving many of these promises again and again in very difficult circumstances." He opened to a page so I could see the various dates he had written adjoining special verses, such as 2/12/46; again 7/20/52; and again 10/9/68 etc.

He continued, "It seems in each new experience, God gives me an enlargement of a promise. It utterly amazes me. I am sure I will continue to prove many of these promises again until I see Him face to face."

As he turned from page to page he added, "I think I should explain I do not just select verses (promises) at random as they catch my attention. No,I dare not plant my feet (so to speak) on a verse until He has specially quickened it to me. Then it moves from being truth on a page to become light in my spirit. In this way I can wait patiently for God to fulfill a verse. You see, when I think I am proving Him in His Word, it is really God who is proving me."

Here is an example: The following story reached the Free World a few years ago from behind the Iron curtain when Secret Police imprisoned a Christian worker. Shortly after his arrest they brought him from his cell into their interrogation room. There, he found a Secret Police officer and a doctor sitting at the interrogation table. Lying open on the table was a Bible. The Christian prisoner was ordered to take a seat and the interrogation began. He was asked: "Do you believe that this book is God's Word?" He answered. "Yes."

The Police official then asked him to read a certain verse. It was Mark 16:18. The Worker read, "...and if they drink any deadly thing, it shall not hurt them."

"Do you believe this part of the Bible, too?" the officer demanded. The Christian replied, "Yes."

The officer then placed a filled glass on the table, explaining, "In this glass there is a strong poison. If the book is true, as you insist, it won't hurt you. To show you we don't play, watch this." The officer brought in a large dog and had the dog drink of the liquid. In a very few moments the dog was lying dead on the floor. The officer looked at the Christian and asked. "Do you still claim this book you call 'God's Word' is true?"

The Christian again answered, "Yes, it is God's Word. It is true."

"Then drink the entire glass!" shouted the communist officer, with the doctor looking on.

The Christian then knew this was the supreme test. He asked for permission to pray before drinking. They granted permission. He knelt down before the table, took the glass in his hand and prayed for his family—that they might remain steadfast in their faith.

He prayed for the communist officer and the doctor, that they might find God and become Christians also. Then, closing his prayer, he added, "Oh, Lord Thou seest how they have challenged Thee. I am ready to die, But I believe in Thy Word that nothing shall happen to me. Should Your plan be different, I am ready to meet Thee. My life is in your hands as you will. May Thy will be done."

With that, he lifted the glass and drank it down.

The communist officer and the doctor were surprised. They didn't expect him to do this, feeling he would surely break first. They watched for him to collapse, as the dog had.

Moments passed into minutes. Minutes seemed to be hours. Complete silence filled the room. Everyone was waiting for the inevitable death.

Then, after several long minutes, the doctor made the first move. He took the arm of the Christian and felt his pulse. It was normal. He looked for other symptoms. There were none.

Expressing amazement and astonishment, he continued his examination, but could find no trace of harm whatsoever. As the examination continued, the doctor became more amazed. Finally, he slumped into his seat, paused a moment, reached into his pocket and removed his Party card, tore it in half and threw it on the floor.

Next, he reached out for the Bible, held it and said, "From today, I will also believe this book. It must be true. I, too, am ready to believe this Christ who did this thing before my eyes."

In this proving of God's Word, the Christian worker was also proved. Both were vindicated. Somehow, I imagine my heavenly Father was looking upon this incident with His smile of approval. You can be sure this Christian worker could place a date beside this verse in his Bible. We are sobered as we recognize how great is the enmity in man against God and His Word. Yet, in such times of crisis God will demonstrate that He is faithful to His own Word.

FATHER, it is no wonder our Lord Jesus boldly announced: "...until heaven and earth disappear, not the smallest letter, nor the least stroke of a pen, will by any means disappear from the Law until everything is accomplished." Matt. 5:18 NIV. What high esteem You have placed on Your word! I do not have dying grace now, but I know that when I need it, You will supply all I need,...even as You did to Your servant who drank the glass of poison. Amen!

"For it is a good thing that the heart be established with grace." (Heb. 13:9)

Crisis of the Will

A BASHFUL YOUNG FARMER . . . out in the West, who was utterly unfamiliar with religious meetings, was challenged by Dr. H. C. Mabie to come to a prayer meeting that evening in a neighboring farmhouse and openly confess Christ. The young man replied "I never could stand up and talk in that way before people, even though I wanted to; it would kill me to do it."

"Well," Dr. Mabie replied, "die then... Christ commands the impossible... He commands you to confess him before men, and I shall expect you to do it tonight, even though you die in doing it."

To the meeting that timid young man came. As he rose to his feet, laboring as if he were Atlas lifting the world on his shoulders—the very effort crushing him—he confessed with his mouth "Jesus is Lord." Before he sat down, he was thanking God for the new life. By faith he had fulfilled the principle of "This do, and thou shalt live."

Some might argue that Dr. Mabie should have shown this young man how to believe instead of stipulating this condition of confession. However, it was divine wisdom that led this seasoned soul-winner to press the issue at the very point where the Spirit of God was already at work in this young man. Dr. Mabie did not make conversion easy. Facing him squarely, he insisted upon the thing impossible—the thing most difficult for him to do. The reasoning of his head was ruling, when he insisted it would kill him to do it; yet his heart obeyed the impossible—he died, as it were, and lived anew.

In circles where religious softness reigns it is often said: "Well, you know, God is very kind and loving; He would never ask anyone to do anything he could not do. Such folk understand little of man's heart rebellion to the ways of God. The Lord always faced the rebel with some (impossible) obedience. He brought souls face to face with some issue that exposed their controversy with God.

The battle is the same today, for God is still testing men by such issues that confront the will. Since Adam, every man has gone astray and turned to his own way. Those who present the Gospel must cross man's will, bring him face to face with that thing which (seems to) well-nigh paralyze him, yet thereby bring him to submission.

In over fifty years of dealing with hundreds of seeking hearts, I have discovered, if I listen attentively long enough, God will uncover that point where they are in controversy with Him. As I look back it has become ever more apparent that each solid conversion has been an issue of Lordship: will I make Jesus Lord, or am I still doing my own thing in my own way?

While listening to a young lady unfold doubts she had about God's way of handling a situation, I simply asked, "Do you have a constant struggle with your father?" In dismay she responded, "Yes I do–but what has that to do with my problem?" It took some time, but my spirit was sensing this was her critical issue. If she would humble herself before her father and submit to him, God could help her. She finally acknowledged that doing this was "going to kill her". The next day she phoned to tell me the blessing that resulted when she had obeyed what we had considered. She explained, "I am a new person, and for the first time I know that I am really the Lord's."

My niece was riding with me to a summer youth conference, and as we approached the grounds, she confided to me: "One thing I'll never do is go to the altar. I can be saved any place I choose." She was not aware that I rarely give the kind of public invitation to which she was alluding to. Yet I knew in my heart she had just exposed that point of controversy she was setting up with God. (Yes, I am greatly concerned about the folks who put their trust in a "trip to the altar" instead of meeting some governmental issue in their controversy with God. But I did not tell her!) For I knew that before the week was over, she must bow to that issue. She did, and Christ became her Lord.

Is it possible the reader has been guilty of this same folly? You have secretly had your own way of insisting, "one thing I'll never do..." Only the Holy Spirit can uncover what has hindered you from submitting your will to the Lord Jesus. It is quite possible some believer has been stalled in his/her walk, because there is a secret controversy over an issue of obedience. Could I listen long enough, would I be able to uncover that hidden issue of controversy you have with God?

I remember Harold, a respected farmer who was an elder in his rural Presbyterian church. During a series of meetings I was staying in his home. One night he confided to me that he was constantly being reminded about a pair of tire chains. He explained the first time he used them in a blizzard they fell apart. When he took the chains back to the store, he insisted he would not pay for them. When I asked him how long ago this had happened, he smiled—"Oh I suppose about fifteen years ago."

I shook my head in disbelief and asked him, "You mean you have allowed this foolish struggle in your heart all these years, over a fifteen dollar pair of chains?" I said no more. Almost immediately he seemed to know what the Lord wanted him to do.

The next night he came in late to the meeting. Just before I stood up to speak, he announced boldly. "Today I went to (........) and paid for a set of chains. Would you believe my chains have fallen off." Indeed they had! Everyone watched with amazement. During the next 20 years we saw Harold grow in wisdom and lead that church, lead his family, and become a spiritual pillar in the community.

If we had more room, I could tell you my own personal stories of times I allowed a secret controversy with God to become a shadow that hindered my fellowship. I know by experience how one can disguise a controversy with vain excuses. But God always knows the issue, and would never let me off the hook until I obeyed.

"...be ye doers of the word, and not hearers only, deceiving your own selves.

But whoso looks into the perfect law of liberty, and continues therein, he being not a forgetful hearer, but a doer of the word, this man shall be blessed. (Jas. 1:25)

FATHER, it is possible there is someone now reading these words who needs to face some "step of obedience." Strangely the Holy Spirit has maneuvered us to this point. Someone will either obey, or they will continue in their hidden controversy. God does offer His grace... AND THEN PEACE.

Yes, I do thank YOU for exposing my heart. Right now I confess the issue has been..........................Amen!

The Joy of Grace-Giving

IT WAS ALMOST FIFTY YEARS AGO. . .
that I first heard Oswald J. Smith explain to us, a crowd of Youth
For Christ directors, how God called him to... **Grace-full Giving.**
It was an experience that wholly changed his life. To this day I
have not forgotten his testimony and living example.

Oswald J. Smith explains that early in his ministry he had just
begun to pastor a small church. At the time, this church was having their Annual Missionary Convention, something entirely new
to him. Seated on the platform, he looked on in interest as ushers
went up and down the aisles handing out envelopes. Then he was
more amazed as an usher came and handed an envelope to him.
Smith explains:

"As I held the envelope I read: 'In dependence upon God I
will endeavor to give toward the Missionary Work of the Church
$_____ during the coming year.'

"I had never read such a statement before... I started to pray.
I said, 'Lord God, I can't do anything. You know I have nothing
in my pocket. This church only pays me $25.00 a week. I have a
wife and child to keep. We are trying to buy our home and everything is sky-high in price.' All that was very true. The First World
War was on.

" 'I know that,' the Lord said. 'Well then,' I continued, 'that set-
tles it. I have nothing to give and I cannot give anything.' I will
never forget what the Lord said: 'I am not asking you for what you
have.'

" 'You are not asking me for what I have, Lord?

" 'Then what are you asking?'" I replied.

" 'I am asking you for a Faith-Offering. How much can you trust
Me for?'

" 'Oh, Lord,' I exclaimed, 'that's different. How much can I
trust You for?' I thought He might say $5.00 or perhaps even
$10.00. Once in my life I had given $5.00 for missions. Once I had
given $3.00. I waited for His answer.

"Presently it came. God did not speak to me in an audible voice,
but He might just as well have done so. I was scarcely conscious of
the congregation as I sat there with my eyes closed, listening to the
Voice of God. The answer came: 'Fifty dollars.'

" 'Fifty dollars!' I exclaimed. 'Why, Lord, that is two weeks' salary. How can I get $50.00?' Again the Lord spoke and it was still the same amount.

"Now, how I ever paid it I don't know to this day. All I know is that every month I had to pray for $4.00; and every month God sent it in some miraculous way. At the end of the year I had paid the entire amount—$50.00.

"I received such a blessing, and there came to my heart such a fullness of the Spirit; it was such a thrill, that as I paid the final amount, I realized that this faith-giving had been one of the greatest experiences of my life.

"So great was the spiritual blessing because I had given a Faith Offering—I had trusted God for a certain amount, I had given in a Scriptural way—that the next year at the Convention, I doubled the amount and gave $100.00. And from that day to this I have been sending on thousands upon thousands of dollars to the Bank of Heaven. If I had waited until I had it, I never would have had it. But I gave—when I didn't have it; I gave a Faith Offering; God honored it."

Because Oswald J. Smith's life and ministry date back so many years ago, let me explain that this beloved man eventually became the pastor of a large church in Toronto, Canada, that has given and given and given to missionary work. In his generation the evangelical world has marveled at his story—the pastor who became a unique demonstration of grace-giving, many years before the modern-day prosperity message.

THIS KIND OF GIVING IS A MATTER OF VISION

Back in the 1940's oil was discovered in South Central Oklahoma. It seemed there was so much oil in that location that every well would be a gusher. Suddenly farmers were becoming fabulously wealthy overnight. One Christian farmer's land was situated in the very middle of what appeared to be a gigantic oil pool.

When the company erected the first drilling rig on his property, the man prayed a very "religious" prayer. He said, "Lord, You know how much I love You and I don't want anything to get in the way of my serving You, so I'm asking that You govern how much oil is found by how much You can trust me."

Due to the ideal location of his property, this man should have had the best producing wells in the county but it was just the contrary; the wells on his property were dribblers, barely bringing in enough to pay for their maintenance even though wells all around him were gushers.

I realize there would be some who are quick to admire this seemingly godly prayer and the Lord's intervention to protect this farmer from greed. Surely, gaining any amount of money is not worth losing your heavenly reward. Many would insist that God really answered his prayer.

Could it be God didn't answer his "religious" prayer, but He honored the man's small measure of faith! What if this man had understood grace-giving as O.J. Smith taught, and he immediately determined to give 90% of the returns to the Lord's work. If he had caught the vision that he must not merely be the object of God's blessing, but he must become a channel for blessing, he could have supported kingdom needs around the world.

I know the dangers of money and the deceitfulness of the heart, but I am convinced too many of God's people have not grasped the Abrahamic promise: "I will bless you and make you a blessing."

If that promise is so dangerous that we dare not claim its full value, we are destined for a lifetime of limitation. No, I am convinced that way back in those days when the tithe was initiated, God planned for His people to give free-will offerings—which are beyond the requirement of the tithe.

So, it is not a matter of Old Testament or New Testament giving, it is whether we are living beyond the smaller window (of duty) or experiencing the blessing of free-will offerings unto God. I include this story because there are many readers who have locked themselves into the tithing box. Yes, God has wonderfully blessed your diligence in tithing ten percent. That is good, yet there is always something much better.

I would like to encourage you to consider the larger window, even as O.J. Smith did, when he began trusting God for an increased grace-offering—far beyond the ten percent.

Of course, if one is satisfied with receiving the smaller blessing then continue giving as you have. But if

Grace-Offering:	
Tithe:	• Privilege
• Required	• Proportionate
• Specified	• Great Joy and
• Much Blessing	MORE Blessing
Mal. 3:8-10	2 Cor. 8:1-15
	9:1-15

your heart longs to become a greater blessing unto God, then listen to how the Apostle Paul exhorts the Corinthian church: that grace-giving should be characterized by (—the attitude is more important than the amount):

Cheerfulness (2 Cor. 9:7)	Liberality (2 Cor. 8:2)
Sacrifice (2 Cor. 8:2-3)	Eagerness (2 Cor. 8:4;7-8)
Willingness (2 Cor. 8:12; 9:2)	Integrity (2 Cor. 2-21)
Purposeful (2 Cor. 9:7)	Proportionate (2 Cor. 8:3,11)

Consider this exhortation from Pastor Norm Willis:

"When Jesus told us to 'store up treasures in heaven,' it was not so He could amass a huge supply, then redistribute it all equally. He told us to store it up for we will each have our individual level (measure) of wealth... determined by our steps of obedience and (eternal) investment."

"What I am addressing is (not our salvation, but) our level of wealth once we get to heaven. The fact we are urged to store up treasures indicates there will be some form of economic trade in heaven. The currency of eternity will not be dollars and cents,

...but it will be the currency of a good name (Prov.22:1),
...the currency of relationship (Phil.3:7-8),
...the currency of faith (John 2:5),
...the currency of wisdom (Prov.8:18), and
...the currency of the Holy Spirit (Eph.1:13-14).

"Those who will be 'rich' in eternity will be those who have sown to eternal principles. So, as an eternal investment advisor, I counsel you to invest in currency that is transferable. Do not give yourself to the food that spoils, but for the food that endures to eternal life." (N.W.)

FATHER, too long I have lived with a mind-set that limited me from giving more and more. I want to ask You to enlarge my heart, and then enlarge my measure of faith. I have been blessed; now I want to become a channel of blessing. I am asking You to help me during this coming year to give more, in a discerning way, to those who are wisely building Your kingdom—and not their own kingdom.

"As he had begun, so He would also finish in you the same grace also... Therefore as ye abound in everything, in faith, and utterance and knowledge, and in all diligence, and in your love to us, see THAT YE ABOUND IN THIS GRACE ALSO."

Proving God's Faithfulness

I CAN STILL RECALL my mother's surprise and pleasure as she opened a carton of canning jars made by the Kerr company and found a most unusual tract: God's Cure for Poverty. I do not remember if mother read the tract to me, but recently (now seventy years later) I discovered this most unusual story of Alexander Kerr and the circumstances of that tract.

At the age of 14 Kerr was converted under the ministry of D.L. Moody and joined the Presbyterian church. Some years later he read a book that totally changed his life. It was the story of the patriarch Jacob who made a vow to God: *"Of all that Thou hast given me, I will surely give the tenth unto Thee"* (Gen. 28:22)

Kerr was greatly impressed how God blessed Jacob when he returned home after 20 years with Uncle Laban, and he had become one of the richest men of the East—all as a result of keeping this covenant with the Lord.

Though it was with some doubts, yet a sincere desire to test this promise in the Bible, Kerr made a special covenant to set aside a certain percentage of his income for the work of the Lord. At that time he had a mortgage on his little home, owed many obligations, and was burdened with many financial worries. However he determined to prove God as Jacob had: (Prov. 3:9, 10; Lev. 27:3-32; Gen. 14:20 and 13:2—especially Mal. 3:7-18).

Within three months after Mr. Kerr began to tithe, unexpected and unforeseen blessing came to him–so much so that it seemed to him that God had opened his eyes to behold His love and amazing faithfulness to fulfill His promises in regard to giving.

That same year, with very little capital, yet a strong conviction that God's promises needed to be tested, he organized the Kerr Glass Manufacturing Company which later became one of the largest firms producing canning jars in the United States. It was in San Francisco that he manufactured these jars at the time of the great Frisco earthquake All his assets were invested in this enterprise when suddenly the terrible quake hit San Francisco. Immediately his friends came to announce their worst fears:

"Kerr, you are a ruined man." His quick response was, "I don't believe it; if I am, then the Bible is not true; I know God will not go back on His promises." He sent a wire to San Francisco and received the following reply: "Your factory is in the heart of the fire, and undoubtedly is destroyed. The heat is so intense we will be unable to move in to find out anything more for a few days."

What a time of testing this was! Yet his faith never wavered, for he was standing on Mal. 3:11: "I will rebuke the devourer for your sakes, and he shall not destroy the fruit of your ground." He continued unmoved for an entire week and then a second telegram arrived saying:

"Everything for a mile and a half on all sides of the factory has burned, BUT YOUR FACTORY IS MIRACULOUSLY SAVED!" Mr. Kerr immediately boarded a train for the West. When he arrived he discovered the fire had raged on all sides of his factory, creeping up to the wooden fence surrounding the building– and even scorching it. Though oil was used for fuel and this building was the most inflammable in the area, nothing had burned, and not a single glass jar was cracked by the earthquake or fire!

To everyone it was the most visible miracle of God's protecting power demonstrated to a man who believed God's tithe-promise would never be broken by any circumstances.

It was in 1912 Mr. Kerr wrote this first leaflet entitled God's Cure for Poverty, and this was followed by another: God's Money Rule for Your Financial Prosperity." It was one of these tracts placed in every case of jars that my mother found when she opened the carton.

We must be careful to recognize with Kerr it was principle-living that governed his life–not merely his confidence in tithing. He had come to know the God who designed the principles. During his life- time every business in which he was involved tithed. It is reported the returns from his investment were so great he incorporated a special fund for sharing Gospel tracts, Testaments and literature around the world.

Thousands have marveled how this man rose from poverty to millions–all because he believed that God would honor his promise. While it is true that Kerr stood on the tithe-promise and God honored His word, let us also recognize that Kerr moved from being an object of God's blessing to become a channel for God's blessing; he moved from mere legal duty (tithing) to the delight of grace-giving.

Whatever terms we use to express this, it is my own conviction that God is continually looking for those who will not be confined to living in the smaller window, but will allow God to use them as a demonstration of the overflow of blessing that comes by living in the larger window.

FATHER, I thank You for allowing me to know and observe some men and women from the past, and some today, who have allowed You to use them as You did Mr. Kerr. With one voice they all celebrate Your goodness, and rejoice in singing:
    To God be the GLORY—great things He has done!

In Beholding Grace, We are Becoming...

STEVEN MCVEY TELLS ABOUT. . . a young woman who lived in the inner city projects whose life was transformed in a wonderful way. Jackie had lived a hard life for many years. She was a drug addict who sometimes sold her body to men to sustain her habit. Some might have blamed it on her upbringing, which had been anything but normal. From the time she was a child, the men in her life had abused and exploited her. Now, as an adult, she trusted no man. None! She was callused! Her language was unusually foul for a woman. She despised men.

A Christian man was ministering in her community when he met her one day. He smiled and said, "Hello." Jackie rudely frowned at Don and immediately turned away. However, Don was persistent. Day after day he came to minister to her neighbors and each day he smiled and spoke to Jackie.

After a while, she actually began to think that maybe—just maybe, this guy was sincerely nice. Then the thought would rush into her mind, "But why would he have any interest in me; what does he want?" However, despite her skepticism and suspicions about his kindness, she gradually began to respond to him a little more each day, until finally she was having conversations with Don.

As weeks turned into months, Jackie began to realize something. Don was interested in her as a lady, not in an inappropriate way. He seemed to genuinely care for her in the way that a man loves a woman with a purity that she had only dreamed about. Could it be that what she was feeling might be true? Did he really *love* her (for herself) as it seemed?

As the thought of being the recipient of this wonderful man's love took root in her mind, Jackie began to change. First, she found that she didn't want to use foul language when she talked to him. She began to anticipate his visits each day and would get dressed up, put on her makeup and even used perfume. She *wanted* to be pleasing to him. He had never criticized her looks or behavior. To the contrary, from the beginning Don had accepted her just like she was. That itself motivated her to want to change.

As Don shared his love with Jackie day after day, she bloomed. Little by little, her life was transformed from a hardened, drug addicted prostitute into a real lady. The change didn't happen because Don pointed out all her faults—he didn't. She wasn't transformed into a lady because it was what she thought she *ought* to do. His love motivated her to *want* to become the lady she was created to be. He didn't lay religious rules on her; he just loved her and his relationship with her caused the great change in her— from inside to outside.

When I read about Jackie, I thought about myself. Why does Jesus love *me?* He never criticizes, never tells me that I have to change to be loved by Him. He just loves me right where I am, no matter what I'm doing or not doing. It's amazing. Sometimes I don't even love me, but I know He does. (SM)

Consider! What motivated Don's gracious actions toward Jackie? I am pressed to ask this question. Could I have done this without a special measure of God's grace? Perhaps not! I am convinced that this goes way beyond what we have called enabling grace. This was God's very special grace. God was looking for a platform on which He could demonstrate the power of His grace—when directed toward a most wretched life. So He chose Jackie to be the object, and He chose Don to become the channel of His grace.

*We have used stories that illustrate God's prevenient grace, (grace before we are even aware of our need).
*We have used stories to illustrate God's saving grace, (grace when we trust Him as Lord and Savior).
*We have used stories that illustrate God's enabling grace, (grace as we approach impossible situations in life), now
*We considered stories that illustrate God's special grace, (grace flowing through as we become vessels of purpose)

THANK YOU FATHER, for showing this larger window of Your grace. When Noah found grace—it was a special grace according to purpose. When Daniel, Joseph, Esther, Ruth, and Job found grace—it was a very special grace according to Divine purpose. This gives me a new confidence. When you call someone to become a demonstrator of grace, You provide special grace. The Enemy might seek to taunt me in my weakness, but I have read.

My Grace is sufficient for thee: for my strength is made perfect in (your) weakness.

Four Aspects of God's Mercy

The Larger Window of Mercy

Providential Mercy	Redemptive Mercy	Selective Mercy	Expressive Mercy
Psalms 119:64	Luke 18:13	Romans 9:15	Matthew 5:7
Psalms 145:9	Luke 1:78	Exodus 33:19	Luke 6:36

PROVIDENTIAL MERCY. Long before we have recognized God's dealing in the affairs of men, His mercy has been demonstrated toward all creation. Why? In His very nature God is compassionate. In many of these stories we shall see that mercy is not something He does, but mercy is His character unveiled.

REDEMPTIVE MERCY. In not giving man the consequences he rightfully deserves, God awakens man to recognize His goodness. It is in that unexplainable moment that the rebellious sinner truly appreciates God's mercy toward him. Actually, the further we progress in our spiritual walk the more we become aware of His mercy. We see an example of this in the old Puritan saint, Thomas Hooker, as he approached death. Those around his bedside said, "Brother Hooker, you are going to receive your reward." "No, no! he breathed, "I am going to receive mercy!" The ripe years of maturity had sharpened his insights to appreciate God's nature more than what he might get.

SELECTIVE MERCY. It still remains an enigma to all God's children why sometimes God intervenes, yet at other times He appears indifferent. Who can explain why He repeatedly announces: "I will show mercy on whom I will show mercy." Surely as long as we look up at the underside of the tapestry, we are puzzled. But some day when we sit with him and view from the larger heavenly viewpoint, we will appreciate the lovely pattern He is weaving. Then we will acknowledge that His "selective mercy" really was fulfilling a divine purpose.

EXPRESSIVE MERCY. If God's highest goal is to use every thing in this universe as a platform for revealing Himself, then it is natural that each of us should choose to become living models for expressing and extolling the wondrous mercy of God. What a privilege that we should be invited to participate in this Grand Demonstration!

A Song in the Night

FOR HIS CHRISTIAN WITNESS. . .
John had been sentenced to thirteen years' imprisonment in a
Communist prison. After about ten years serving time, he committed some small misdemeanor and was sent to an isolation
block. Here, complete silence reigned, and this absolute solitude
was miserable.

John became so depressed in spirit that one day he cried to the
Lord wanting to die. What was the use of living, anyway? Ten
years of suffering in the general block and now this! He felt—
and who can blame him—that it was more unbearable than he
could take. But after a while, he pulled himself together. Feeling
thoroughly ashamed of his lapse in faith, he began very softly to
sing to himself the hymn, *"Count your blessing"*—

> *"When upon life's billows you are tempest tossed,*
> *When you are discouraged, thinking all is lost,*
> *Count your many blessings, name them one by one,*
> *And it will surprise you what the Lord has done."*

As he sang quietly, he could hear the fellow in the cell next
door, pacing up and down, backwards and forwards. Suddenly,
John could restrain himself no longer and he burst into loud
song, realizing most surely that the guards would come and beat
him. Who knows—perhaps they might even pound him to death!
Maybe this was the way in which God was going to answer his
prayer! As these thoughts were flashing through his mind, his
brain was also registering that the prisoner's footsteps next door
had stopped. He continued singing

> *"Are you ever burdened with a load of care?*
> *Does the cross seem heavy you are called to bear?*
> *Count your many blessings, every doubt will fly,*
> *And you will keep singing as the days go by."*

John sang his way through the verses of the hymn, becoming
louder and more confident with each chorus, listening with one
ear for the jangling keys of the warder and his angry, heavy footsteps. At any moment he expected the door to be opened and the
beatings with the heavy bludgeon to begin.

> *"So, amid the conflict, whether great or small,*
> *Do not be disheartened, God is over all;*

73

Count your many blessings, angels will attend,
Help and comfort give you to your journey's end."

But nothing happened! No guards came! All was silent except for the noise of a heavy plop on the floor in the next cell. The poor chap, thought John, must have collapsed. Perhaps he had even died.

Weeks went by. John, having finished serving his time in solitary confinement, was taken back to the general prison block. There, he at least had company, and the diet was a little better than the stale bread and water he had been living on for the past three months.

One evening as he was sitting down after the day's work, he felt so very grateful to God for preserving his life. He began to hum *"Count your blessings"* to himself. He had not gotten very far when he felt a heavy hand on his shoulder. Turning, he saw another prisoner standing above him.

"Listen," the man said. "Were you in Cell Number 11 in the isolation block at such-and-such a time?"

"I was," replied John.

"I heard you," said the man with mounting excitement. "I could hear you! You sang that tune you're now humming! And I heard those words. I was just about to kill myself. I had made a noose out of my underwear... fixed it up to the ceiling. Just before you sang, I stopped my pacing around in my cell, stood on the chair, and put my head in the noose. Then you started to sing. You sang louder and louder. The words came through stronger and stronger. I was waiting for the guards to come and silence you for good. Then, I decided that if there was someone in this prison who could sing fearlessly like that about a God who cared—then life must be worth living after all. I took my head out of the noose and dropped to the floor. Now, tell me about this God and this faith you have, because I want it too!"

John was thrilled! He told the man about the love of God and the salvation offered through Jesus Christ. Then and there, he led him to personally trust the Lord Jesus as his Savior. Today those men are not only free, but serving together in a church behind the iron curtain.

Father, I am reminded of Paul and Silas singing praises in the middle of the night... Though they had been falsely charged as trouble makers, You turned this for the salvation of the jailer and all his house. Out of each night of adversity there is a morning of joy. You touched the jailer who "...brought them to his own house, set meat before them, and rejoiced" (Acts 16:34).

God Was There

DAVID A SEAMANDS EXPLAINS:

BETTY and her husband came to counsel with me. I knew that they were a deeply committed Christian couple preparing for Christian service, and that they had a solid marriage. However, recently there had been some relational difficulties between them and an increasing sense of depression on Betty's part. Her tears flowed freely that first time we met together—tears which surprised her. She thought she had turned them off many years ago, but now they seemed to turn themselves on, uncontrollably and embarrassingly.

When Betty came back the second time, she began to share her story with me. Her parents had been forced to get married because her mother was pregnant with her. It was an undesired marriage and Betty had been unwanted. (May I just say parenthetically that if this is true of your life, sometime you need to come to peaceful terms with it.)

When Betty was three and a half, her mother became pregnant again. However, Betty's father had impregnated another woman at about the same time. This led to serious conflict and finally to divorce. Betty's memory of all this was incredibly clear. She vividly remembered that final day when her father walked out the door and left home. She remembered being in her own little cribbed in the room when it happened, hearing the vicious quarrel and the terrifying moment when he left. It had left an aching, malignant core of pain deep within her. It was while we were in the midst of re-experiencing that incident during a time of prayer for the healing of her memories, that the Lord took us right back into that crib.

Our Lord Jesus can do that, you know, because all time is present with Him. He is the One who said, "Before Abraham was, I am" (Jn 8:58). Our memories are all there before Him who is the Lord of all time. During that healing time, Betty uttered a wracking, wrenching cry of pain which had been buried for many years. I said to her, "Betty, if you could have said something to your father from your crib, at that moment—what would you have said?" And suddenly the Holy Spirit brought back up into her memory exactly what she had felt in that moment of desolation.

And she cried out, not in the voice of a young adult, but with the sobs of a three-and-a-half year old, "Oh, Daddy, please don't leave me!" And all the terror and the pain of that moment came out "with sounds too deep to be uttered."

Later, as we prayed together, it dawned on me that if we were to translate Christ's cry of dereliction from the cross ("My God, My God, why hast Thou forsaken me!") into a paraphrase for a child, we couldn't improve on Betty's words: "Daddy, please don't leave me!"

And suddenly, I realized that because of what Jesus experienced on that cross, He understands the cries heard so often in our day, the cries of millions of little children, "Daddy," or "Mommy, please don't leave me!" But they do leave. And the Wounded Healer understands those cries and is touched with the feelings of those children.

This was the beginning of a profound healing in Betty's life. However, I wanted her to experience the ultimate wholeness promised in Romans 8:28. So we talked about trying to understand the meaning of her life. Where was God when she began life itself?

Had she made peace with the circumstances of her birth through an unwanted pregnancy? She said she hadn't.

I felt led to give her a strange assignment, one I've given out only a few times in all my counseling years. I said, "Betty, I am going to give you some homework and I want you to spend time meditating and praying about it. I want you to imagine the very moment of your conception. Imagine that particular time when one cell of life from your father broke into the living cell of your mother, and you came into existence. That's when you broke into human history. As you think about that, ask yourself one question: where was God at that moment?"

Betty took her assignment seriously. When we met one week later, she told me what had happened: "You know, the first two or three days, I really thought this whole thing was crazy. The only thing I could think of was a verse of Scripture which kept coming to my mind, 'In sin did my mother conceive me.' But about the third day when I was reluctantly meditating on it, I began to cry. But it was a different cry than usual. A prayer was welling up from way down inside me, and I wrote it down."

She handed it to me, and with her permission I share it with you:

Oh God, my Heart leaps with the thought that You, my loving Father, have never forsaken me. You were there when I was conceived in earthly lust. You looked upon me with a Father's love even then. You were thinking of me in my mother's womb, planning in Your divine knowledge the person I was to become, remolding me in Your image.

Knowing the pain in store, You gave me a mind that would pull me above the hurt, until in Your own timing You could heal me.

You were there when my mother gave birth to me, looking on in tenderness, standing in the vacant place of my father. You were there when I cried the bitter tears of a child whose father abandoned her. You were holding me in Your arms all the while, rocking me gently in Your soothing love.

Oh, why did I not know of Your presence? Even as a child I was blind to Your love, unable to know it in its depth and breadth.

God, my dear, dear Father, my heart had turned to frost, but the light of Your love is beginning to warm it. I can feel again. You have begun to work in me a healing miracle. I trust You and I praise You. Your goodness and mercy have been with me always. Your love has never left me. And now the eyes of my soul have been open. I see You for who You really are, my true Father. I know Your love and now I am ready to forgive. Please make the healing complete.

Betty had found the final stage of healing when God took all the hurts she gave Him and healed them by His recycling and healing love. But then God put the frosting on the cake—He used Betty as a healed helper.

One Sunday morning I did something in my sermon that I rarely do. With Betty's express permission I used the above story. I disguised details that would identify her, since I knew she would be in the congregation. At the end of the service I invited people to come forward to the altar if they desired to pray for emotional healing.

A large number responded. Betty was seated next to a friend who began to weep profusely during the time of invitation, but who did not go forward. Betty moved closer, and putting her arm around her friend, asked if she would like her to go with her and pray for her. The lady was hesitant, and protested that her problems were too deep and that Betty wouldn't really understand.

Now there took place within Betty a real struggle: she knew what she thought God was asking her to do, and she thought He was asking a little too much! But within minutes she knew what she had to do. So she leaned over and whispered in her friend's ear, "Don't be shocked: I gave Dr Seamands permission to tell that story this morning: you see, I'm Betty!" Her friend looked at her incredulously.

"Yes," she said again, "I'm Betty, and I think I can understand and maybe help " They came forward together and spent a long time sharing and praying. This was the beginning of a healing in the life of Betty's friend. When Betty related it to me, she had the glow of a healed helper. God had truly recycled her hurts into healing and helpfulness! (DAS)

Let us consider again: where was God in Betty's beginning? She was wanted and loved by God, even though her parents might have felt she was an intrusion upon them. All life is precious to Him, for this is according to His Paternal plan and desire for a vast family who will be conformed to the image of His Son. Though sin and lustful desire may produce children, God claims them as part of His creation. He is Source of all life. Never accept the Enemy's lie that you were a mistake. Each of us is wanted and loved by God so much, that He provided redemption for you at the awful cost of giving His Son, Jesus.

We have explained previously (see appendix A) that God is the Source of all life: both the created life we receive from Adam, and uncreated Life which is available to us in Christ Jesus.

FATHER, I now see how You have invaded this human arena to expose the awful lie: many falsely assume they are not wanted or loved. Yes, God is the great Lover of all His creation. It is possible that God has directed you (the reader) to this very moment, and you can look up into your Father's face and announce: I know You wanted me. That matters most. I accept Your healing, now! And I rejoice that You can turn other wounded souls—as they are enlightened—to become a healer of others. May everyone who reads this story accept Your invitation to be available—to enlighten the wounded and hurting. Yes, God, You so loved all Your creation... that You gave... and gave! We are loved very much!

The Smell of Rain

A COLD MARCH WIND DANCED. . . around the dead of night in Dallas as the doctor walked into the small hospital room of Diana Blessing. Still groggy from surgery, her husband David held her hand as they braced themselves for the doctor's news.

That afternoon in March complications had forced Diana, only 24-weeks pregnant, to undergo an emergency caesarean to deliver the couple's new daughter, Danae Lu Blessing. At 12 inches long and weighing only one pound and nine ounces, they already knew she was perilously premature. The doctor's soft words dropped like bombs:

"I don't think she's going to make it," he said, as kindly as he could. "There's only a 10-percent chance she will live through the night, and even then, if by some slim chance she does make it, her future could be a very cruel one."

Numb with disbelief, David and Diana listened as the doctor described the devastating problems Danae would likely face if she survived. She would never walk, she would never talk, she would probably be blind, and she would certainly be prone to other catastrophic conditions from cerebral palsy to complete mental retardation, and on and on.

"No! No!"—was all Diana could say. She and David, with their 5-year-old son Dustin, had long dreamed of the day that they would have a daughter to become a family of four. Now, within a matter of hours, that dream was slipping away.

Through the dark hours of morning as Danae held onto life by the thinnest thread, Diana slipped in and out of sleep, growing more and more determined that their tiny daughter would live— and live to be a healthy, happy young girl.

But David, fully aware of additional dire details of their daughter's chances of ever leaving the hospital alive, knew he must confront his wife with the inevitable. David walked in and said that they needed to talk about making funeral arrangements.

Diana remembers: "I felt so bad for him because he was doing everything to include me in what was going on, but I just wouldn't listen. I couldn't listen.

I said, "No, that is not going to happen, no way! I don't care what the doctors say. Danae is not going to die! One day she will be just fine, and she will be coming home with us!"

As if willed to live by Diana's determination, Danae clung to life hour after hour, with the help of every medical machine and marvel her miniature body could endure. But as those first days passed, a new agony set in for David and Diana.

Because Danae's underdeveloped nervous system was essentially "raw," the lightest kiss or caress only intensified her discomfort. So they couldn't even cradle their tiny baby girl against their chests to offer the strength of their love. All they could do, as Danae struggled alone beneath the ultraviolet light in the tangle of tubes, was to pray that God would stay close to their precious little girl.

They waited patiently for Danae to grow stronger, and as the weeks went by, she did slowly gain an ounce of weight here and an ounce of strength there. At last, when Danae turned two months old, her parents were able to hold her in their arms for the very first time. And two months later, though doctors continued to gently but grimly warn that her chances of surviving, much less living any kind of normal life, were next to zero, Danae went home from the hospital just as her mother had predicted.

Five years later, Danae was a petite, but feisty young girl with glittering gray eyes and an unquenchable zest for life. She showed no signs whatsoever of any mental or physical impairment. Simply, she was everything a little girl could be and more. But that happy note is far from the end of her story.

One blistering afternoon in the summer of 1996 near her home in Irving, Texas, Danae was sitting in her mother's lap in the bleachers of a local ballpark where her brother Dustin's baseball team was practicing. As always, Danae was chattering nonstop with her mother and several other adults sitting nearby when she suddenly fell silent.

Hugging her arms across her chest, Danae asked, "Do you smell that?"

Smelling the air and detecting the approach of a thunderstorm, Diana replied, "Yes, it smells like rain."

Danae closed her eyes again and asked, "Do you smell that?"

Once again, her mother replied, "Yes, I think we're about to get wet. It smells like rain."

Still caught in the moment, Danae shook her head, patted her thin shoulders with her small hands and loudly announced, "No, it smells like Him. It smells like God when you lay your head on His chest." (Amazing! That one so small could recall those beginning days.)

Tears blurred Diana's eyes as Danae then happily hopped down to play with the other children.

Before the rains came, her daughter's words confirmed what Diana and all the members of the extended Blessing family had known, at least in their hearts, all along. During those long days and nights of the first two months of her life, when her nerves were too sensitive for them to touch her, Our Father was holding Danae on His chest, and it is His loving scent that she remembers so well.

This story of Danae has been published many times in many places. Now I have this update as of 12/1/01. The mother, Diana, said that their daughter (now ten and a half) continues to amaze everyone. Full of life and joy, she was out hunting with friends when I called the Blessing home.

In her beginning days, when Danae laid on His breast, she enjoyed God's tender care as a member of Adam's family through creation. Let us be clear: God is the Source of all life–both created and uncreated life. When she was born, our God, who is all-knowing, could look down the corridor of time to see that Danae would one day receive Christ as her Life; then she would person-ally experience God in the relationship of begetting Father.

What a vivid illustration of God's prevenient grace—grace that God extends before we can even personally respond to Him.

FATHER, it is wonderful to know that You were there at my begin-ning, that You are my father in a two-fold way (see appendix A) My inner spirit, now redeemed, calls out to You to say, "Abba Father!" Which means I am entitled to enjoy all the privileges of a son who can sit at Your table. I pray that I might more fully appreciate all this means as we journey together.

APPENDIX A

(1) All people are called the offspring of God (Acts 17:29); therefore, there is a sense in which God is the Father of all men as their Creator. This is simply a creature-Creator basis, and is in no sense a spiritual one.

(2) God is the Father of the nation Israel (Jer. 31:9). Not all Israel were redeemed, so this relationship was both spiritual (with believers) and governmental (with all in Israel, whether believers or not).

(3) God is the Father of the Lord Jesus Christ (Mt 3:17)–both share uncreated Life.

(4) In a very special way God is the Father of those who believe in Christ (Gal. 3:26).Once we were in the family of the First Adam, and possessed created life, but now through Christ, we are born into the family of God, and possess (eternal) uncre-ated Life.

Conversion

SOME OF YOU MAY RECALL. . . the world-famous poem which was circulated so widely among the service men during World War II. During those years the writer received some 600,000 letters from all over the world explaining heart-warming circumstances resulting from the poem.

In writing to the editor who had just published it, Miss Frances Angermayer explains how this poem had its birth. She writes:

I thought you might like to hear about some of the amazing responses which have come to me. I am told that the poem was found on many of our dead soldiers (also those of the enemy). I have cried by the hour over the many stories told me by parents of boys who lost their lives. Many found the poem among the personal effects of their loved ones, when things were returned.

Chaplains told me about finding it clutched in the hands of boys killed during the Normandy beachhead battle. I have never gotten over it, and never shall. I thank God every day that some little effort of mine helped those boys who were dying or afraid before they went into battle. Even this long (1951) after the war, I have been stunned at the reaction in letters from various parts of the world explaining how the poem helped them. I am humbled!

I was awakened in the early hours of June 3, 1943. It was a warm night, and I was unable to sleep. A prayer eased my troubled thoughts for my brother, Corp. Glenn Virtue, who had put in almost four years of service in the Southwest Pacific. Then I thought of the other servicemen far from home, and I wondered what a soldier might do in time of danger if he could not pray!

I arose, folded a bath towel under my portable typewriter to dull the taps, and wrote swiftly the first version of the poem. I called it a "Soldier's Conversion." It was written in about twenty minutes. I pulled it from the typewriter and made a few minor changes with a pencil. Then I retyped it, changing the title to "A Conversion." In less than an hour from the time I began to write the poem, with two or three more changes, I typed the final copy.

A Conversion

Look, God I have never spoken to You...
But now... I want to say, 'How do You do."
You see, God, they told me You didn't exist...
And like a fool... I believed all of this.

Last night from a shell-hole, I saw Your sky...
I figured right then, they had told me a lie.
Had I taken time to see the things You made,
I'd known they weren't calling a spade a spade...

I wonder, God, if You'd shake my hand.
Somehow... I feel that You will understand.
Funny... I had to come to this hellish place,
Before I had the time to see Your face...

Well, I guess there isn't much more to say.
But I'm sure glad, God, I met You today.
I guess the "zero hour" will soon be here.
But I'm not afraid since I know You're near.

The signal!... Well, God... I'll have to go.
I like You lots—This I want You to know...
Who knows... I may come to Your House tonight,

Though I wasn't friendly with You before,
I wonder God... if You'd wait at the door...
Look!... I'm crying! Me—Shedding tears!
I wish I'd known You these many years.

Well, I will have to go now, God... goodbye.
Strange!... Since I met You... I'm not afraid to die.

This poem first appeared in Our Sunday Visitor, a religious publication here in Huntington, Indiana. After that, its popularity spread with amazing rapidity. The Associated Press featured it in every large newspaper in the United States. Five million copies were distributed to G.I.'s in almost every nation on earth. More than 250,000 were sent to Jewish servicemen overseas. Since that time it has been translated into nearly every civilized language, and has been read in thousands of churches.

Many readers will, perhaps, question if this was really an adequate calling upon God for salvation. Without getting involved in theological issues of prayer, let us admit that it does come short of what is usually considered the "sinners prayer." But we have been showing how God does hear the desperate cry from the heart. *"Whosoever shall call on the name of the Lord!"*

It would seem there is no acknowledgement of sin, (or is there)? One could wish he was trusting Christ's finished work on the cross as payment for his sin-debt, and then receiving Christ into his life to be his life. How much is one required to know? If the heart is pleading—crying for help, it that enough? Perhaps many of these elements (such as repentance) are hidden in this young soldier's prayer, perhaps quite unrecognized.

During most of my ministry I have insisted that believing required knowing truth (facts). If someone would reply, "I'm a believer!" Then I would usually ask—"what do you believe?" It seems this soldier did yield himself to God. It is important that you *"believe God is, and He is a rewarder of those who diligently seek Him."*

It should be apparent to most everyone, and surely the Bible record is clear, that God's real controversy is with the government of our heart. *"All we like sheep have gone astray...each has turned to his own way."* Since rebellion of the heart is the first issue that God will deal with, then God can clear up the deficient knowledge of the head.

In some of the following stories we shall consider the minimum requirement in the sinner if he is to trust Christ and be saved.

FATHER, I rejoice that You have made the way of salvation so very simple and available. Any heart that cries out in desperation to You, surely You will hear and forgive. I am so thankful that my conversion did not depend on how much I understood, but simply on my crying out to a merciful God. You did hear me. Amen

The Rewards of Mercy

AS A BUGLER. . .
for my boy scout troop and later in my ROTC training, I had often played the "TAPS." But its mournful melody had little meaning to me until I discovered **this story of how** the "TAPS" originated.

It all began in 1862 during the Civil War. A Union Army Captain, Robert Ellicombe by name, was with his men near Harrison's Landing in Virginia. The battle lines were formed. The Confederate Army was on one side of this narrow strip of land. The Union troops faced them on the other. The fighting was intense for both.

During the night, Ellicombe heard the moaning of a soldier who lay mortally wounded on the field. As the pleading sound of suffering drifted to his ears, mercy gripped his heart. He was not sure if it was a Union or Confederate soldier. However, he determined to risk his life and bring the man back for medical treatment. Regardless!

Mercy must rule in this instance! Crawling through the gunfire on his stomach, the Captain reached the stricken soldier and brought him to his own lines. Then he noticed it was a Confederate soldier he had rescued—but the lad had died on the way bringing him to their trench line.

Then as he was lighting a lantern, he suddenly caught his breath. He was numb with shock! In the dim light, he saw the face of the soldier. It was his own son! His boy had been studying music in a Southern school when the war broke out. Without telling his father, he had enlisted in the Confederate Army.

The following morning, the heart-broken father asked his superiors for permission to give his son a full military funeral. His request was partially granted. The Captain had asked if a group of army band members could play a funeral dirge at the gravesite. That part of the request was turned down since he was a Confederate. Nevertheless, out of mercy and respect for the father, they granted a single musician of his choice. The father chose a bugler.

The bugler was asked to play a series of notes that the father had found in his son's pocket. Yes, you guessed right, that series of notes became the haunting melody we now know as "TAPS."

What an unveiling of a father's merciful heart—a mercy that was offered (to an unknown) and received its reward! I can almost hear my heavenly Father saying—"I know how a father-heart grieves."

Consider! The desperate crying of this dying soldier found two ears. A merciful God in heaven caused an earthly father to hear and respond to this pleading voice. There is no doubt that many on both sides (Union and Confederate) heard this plaintive cry, but God providentially moved his own father to respond.

Some months ago we heard a seminar leader share with pastors how God had awakened him to see the difference between mere asking and desperate crying. This distinction really caught our attention as he explained how God had personally heard his cry most recently, in a time of desperate need. He explained that praying had not seemed to reach God's ear, as did his desperate crying. As he cautiously unfolded how God had sovereignly worked in response to his heart cry, we all knew it was a Rhema word for us. Many of us were at that moment needing very special help from the Lord.

In the Scriptures there are many instances when David is crying out to the Lord. Recall how one time David has been fleeing from king Saul who is seeking his life. David has reached a cave where he is hiding. Suddenly he is aware that King Saul has discovered his location. In desperation David cries out:

"Be merciful unto me, O God, be merciful unto me: for my soul trusteth in thee: yea in the shadow of thy wings will I make my refuge, until these calamities be past over." David continues:

I WILL CRY unto God most high; unto God that performs all things for me. He shall send from heaven, and save me from the reproach of him that would swallow me up. God shall send forth his mercy and truth."
(Ps. 57:1-3)

It is possible that someone now reading this story is facing some impossible crisis. May I suggest that you personally CRY OUT for God to hear and intervene. You may be alone so you can with a loud voice call out. Or you may need to move to some location where you can cry more freely. Do it now! Cry out desperately.

OH FATHER of mercies, we do not know how many times You have already intervened to help us. But we know how you helped David:

"In my distress I cried unto the Lord, and He heard me." (Ps. 120:1)

A Rabbi Learned Why...

A.W. TOZER WRITES:

MY FATHER was 60 years old when he bowed his knee before Jesus Christ and was born again. That was nearly a life-time through which he had sinned, lied and cursed. But when he gave his heart to the Lord Jesus Christ and was converted, the mercy of God that saved him and took him to heaven was no greater than the providential mercy of God that had kept him and endured him—through 60 years of presumption and rebellion.

There is an old story about a Jewish Rabbi, centuries ago who consented to take a weary traveler into his house for a night's rest.

After they had eaten together, the Rabbi said, "You are a very old man, are you not?"

"Yes," the traveler replied. "I am almost a century old."

As they talked, the Rabbi brought up the matter of religion and asked the visitor about his faith and about his relation to God.

"Oh, I do not believe in God," the aged man replied. "I am an atheist."

When the Rabbi heard this, he was infuriated. He rose up, opened the door, and ordered the man from his house.

"I cannot keep an atheist in my house overnight," he reasoned.

The weary old man said nothing but hobbled to the door and stepped out into the darkness. The Rabbi again sat down by his candle to read his Old Testament. Then it seemed he heard a voice saying, "Son, why did you turn that old man out?"

"I turned him out because he is an atheist, and I cannot endure him overnight!"

Then the Rabbi heard God's voice saying, "Son, I have endured him for almost 100 years. Don't you think you could endure him for one night?"

The Rabbi leaped from his chair, rushed out into the darkness, and overtaking the older man, brought him back into his house, treated him like a long lost brother.

It was the **providential** mercy of God that endured the atheist for nearly 100 years. It was this same mercy of God that endured my father as a sinner for 60 years. The same mercy of God endured me through my first 17 years. The Bible plainly declares that God deals with all of us in mercy and that He never violates

His mercy. This explains why David testified, *"The Lord is good to ALL, and his tender mercies are over ALL His works."*

That is why an unrepentant sinner may live to be 100 years old, though he sins against God every moment of his life. He is still a partaker of the providential mercy of God!... It is because of the mercy of God that he is not consumed.

We do believe in justice and we believe in judgment. We believe the only reason mercy triumphs over judgment is that God by a divine, omniscient act of redemption, fixed it so man could escape justice and live in the sea of mercy! The justified man... who believes in Jesus Christ—is born anew and becomes a redeemed child of God

However the unjust man—the unrepentant sinner—lives in mercy now in a lesser degree, but the time will come when he will face the judgment of God. Though he had been kept by the mercy of God from death, insanity, and disease, he can violate that mercy, turn his back on it and walk into judgment one day. Then it is too late! (A.W.T.)

FATHER, more and more I realize how mankind is blessed by Your abundant mercy. I realize that mercy is not something You do, but it is what You are in nature—according to Thy great mercy!
In the past I had mostly emphasized your redemptive mercy; now I recognize your providential mercy to all Your creation. Further, I am awed that You have reasons (hidden to us) for Your selective mercy: (I will show mercy on whom I will show mercy!). It is with great joy that I can join the heavenly choir in singing this glorious anthem of the ages: Your mercy endures unto all generations!

Pursuing Beyond the Ladder

SOMEHOW IN MY. . .
fifty years of ministry, I had failed to appreciate what great lengths the Lord goes to in winning men to Himself. I have often drawn a ladder explaining that in Jesus Christ, God has come all the way down to the bottom rung of the ladder to meet fallen man. I always emphasized how other religions insist that man by his own efforts can climb up to meet God. But the uniqueness of the Christian message is that God has come all the way down to meet helpless man.

However, I had added a rung at the bottom!

Without realizing it, I was insisting that sinners come to Him. They must meet Him at the bottom rung.(Yes, climb up the first rung to acknowledge Him as Lord.) They should seek him and desire Him, want Him to be Lord of their lives. Then, and then only, would He save them.

Then I have made this amazing discovery. In many places in the scripture we see that Jesus is the seeking Savior. He actually leaves the ladder in going out to search for fallen, hurting sinners who are afraid of Him. It is true He bids sinners to "come unto Me," but when they will not come, He moves from the ladder to find them.

The Psalmist boldly declares, "there is none that seeks God—no not one." We are told that the shepherd left the ninety-and nine to seek for that one lost sheep. Remember, Jesus was passing by Zaccheus in the tree, and then went to his house; Jesus went to the well to encounter the woman who had had many husbands; Jesus went to the pool at Bethesda to heal the crippled man.

We are not implying that no one ever came to Jesus. The rich young ruler and Nicodemus came to Him. But for the most part, sinful men were not seeking Him, but were running from Him. So it is quite clear that Jesus came...

•to search out those who were afraid of Him,

•to enlighten those who were deceived,

•to awaken those who were wholly dead toward God,

•to give desire and ability to those who didn't want Him.

Yes, Jesus Christ comes as **the Friend of Sinners** to help all those in the above conditions. What an amazing discovery—that the Friend of Sinners delights to do much **preparatory** work in men's hearts. He comes as a Friend to win hearts and enlighten minds so they will be able to acknowledge His Lordship and receive Him personally as their Savior.

When I discovered how inclusive Jesus was in His friendships, it truly opened the larger window for me:

I had mostly considered His wonderful friendship with friends, like Mary, Martha and Lazarus at Bethany. And to the disciples He spoke: "I say unto you my friends." That was the size of my window.

Yet, we are shown how He was also the friend of publicans and sinners (Lk.7:34). But there is a further surprise to discover that Jesus even called Judas his friend, when he placed a betrayal kiss: "Friend, wherefore art thou come."

Can we doubt that this three-fold friendship issues out of what Jesus is, not out of any worthiness demonstrated in others. In our usual relationships it is a two-way street: we will be friendly with those who are friendly, but with Jesus it is simply a one-way street. He is our friend in spite of us. That is why this gospel is such good news. Let me say it again; like the Hound of Heaven He is seeking the hopeless and helpless, even though they are usually running away and avoiding Him. He not only came down to the bottom, but left the ladder to find you and me. Remember how Jesus found Zaccheus hiding in the tree as He walked by, and announced to him. "This day is salvation come to this house... for the Son of Man is come to seek and to save that which was lost."

HEAVENLY FATHER, I thank You for Your *rich mercy in opening my* eyes and heart to receive this truth, and for *placing in me a greater desire* to go after the lost, to win hearts to Yourself. Help me first of all, to be willing to become the friend of sinners, even as You did. And when they don't respond to my friendship, help me not to become offended, but to continue seeking to win them. Amen!

Catching Men

WATCHMAN NEE EXPLAINS:
In the Gospels the Lord Jesus is presented to us as the **Friend** of sinners. Historically, He was found moving among them as their Friend before He became their Savior. Even before we have reached the point where we are willing—or indeed able—to receive Him as Savior, He first comes to us as a Friend. His personal, friendly encounter is not barred from us. By this means, He provides an open door for us to receive Him as Savior. This is a precious discovery.

(Nee continues), since I saw the Savior as the Friend of sinners, I have seen many unusual and difficult people brought to the Lord. I remember how in one place a young woman came and attacked me, saying that she did not want to be saved. She said she was young, intended to have a good time, did not want to have to leave her ways, and become sedate and sober. For then there would be no joy in life. She insisted that she had no intention of forsaking her sins; she expressed not the least desire for salvation! Eventually, I learned she knew quite a lot about the Gospel. She had been brought up in a missionary school, and she reacted against it.

"Shall we pray?" I asked her, after she had more or less ranted and raved at me for awhile.

"What should I pray?" she asked scornfully.

"I can't be responsible for your prayer," I said, "but I will pray first, and then you can tell the Lord all that you have been saying to me."

"Oh, I couldn't do that!" she exclaimed, somewhat taken aback.

"Yes, you can," I replied. "Don't you know that He is the Friend of sinners?"

This touched her. She did pray—a very unorthodox prayer. From that hour the Lord began to work in her heart. Because, in a couple of days, she was saved!

A striking example of one who came to God without even wanting to be saved is afforded by the experience of an English lady of the last century. One of a wealthy family of good social position, she was well educated, a good musician and an accomplished dancer, and she was both young and beautiful. One night she was invited to a ball. She had a wonderful ball dress specially made for the occasion, and that night she was most sought after by all.

After the ball was over she went home, took off her ball dress and cast it aside. She flung herself down and said, "O God, I have everything I want—wealth, popularity, beauty, youth—and yet I am absolutely miserable and unsatisfied. Christians would tell me that this is a proof that the world is empty and hollow, and that Jesus could save me and give me peace and joy and satisfaction.

"But I don't want the satisfaction that He could give. I don't want to be saved. I hate You and I hate Your peace and joy. But, God, give me what I don't want, and if You can, make me happy!" It is recorded that she got up from her knees a saved woman, and became one who knew the Lord in a deep way.

I affirm once again: all that is needed is an honest heart.

During the many years that I have preached the Gospel in China, many of course have initially understood the way of salvation, many have first of all been convicted of sin, have repented, and have believed. But praise God, there have also been many others who, though they did not in the first place repent or believe, or even consciously desire to be save, yet were persuaded to come honestly to the Lord and make personal contact with Him; and in many of these, too, understanding, conviction, repentance and faith have followed and they have, as a result, been gloriously saved. This gives me confidence to state unequivocally that there is none other condition necessary to being saved except that of being a sinner and being honest enough to say so to the Lord. That condition is enough to allow the Holy Spirit to begin His convicting and transforming work. (W.N.)

FATHER, if honesty of heart is the doorway, then I want to use more wisdom in winning souls, even as Watchman Nee explains. I am sure the Holy Spirit can use His searchlight to penetrate into the darkened hearts of folk all around me. Since He is most willing, I am willing. Together we shall discover how hunger, honesty and humility will bring many into the kingdom. Amen!

God Will Reveal Himself to You!

WHILE I WAS IN CALGARY holding meetings, a woman came into the home where I was staying. A very angry and disturbed person, she explained she had been under great stress for many months. She could not sleep and consumed sedatives in order to complete her Masters program at the University. I gently suggested she needed God in her life. Almost instantly, she erupted like a volcano.

"I don't believe there is a God," she protested. "Besides, if there is a God, I hate Him! He's never helped me," unleashing her abuse and bitterness.

"I know there is a God," I broke in, after listening for a few minutes."I know, because of what He has done in my life. But you do not know that. My God would like to make Himself real to you, if you will let Him."

By now, I was recalling a booklet I had recently read. Would God really be a "Friend to *this* sinner" in order that she might meet Him as her Lord and Savior? Now was the opportunity for God to prove this to *me,* as well as to *her.*

"Would you tell God everything you have told me," I asked, though her anger was still apparent. "Just be open and honestly express your heart. Even your bitterness! Tell Him everything you have told me."

"Why should I pray to a God I don't believe exists?" she retorted. "What kind of fool do you think I am?"

"I know," I continued. "I realize this seems foolish! But I know there is a God Who wants to make Himself known to you. Please listen to me. I am going to pray and ask my God to somehow help you to understand that He exists. And He will respond. He will help you know He exists. In all of your present disappointments and personal bitterness, you can count upon Him to be your Friend. He is even a Friend to help sinners who don't want Him to invade their private lives."

She balked, wincing as I bowed to pray.

"God, I know you hear me when I ask in Jesus name that You make yourself known to this distressed lady. She can't sleep. Can't eat. Can't finish her studies. I know You will meet her here and now as she opens her heart to express in honesty everything she has told me. I thank You, Lord, for hearing me and answering the cry she is making to You."

Somehow, I just knew my God was ready to meet her. The only question now was whether she would call out for His help. Or, would she just 'mouth words' to satisfy me and get me off her back?

"Oh, alright," she blurted out. "I don't believe there is a God who hears, or even cares. But God, if You do exist, if You really do care for people—as this man says, then I challenge You. Help me know. You know how miserable I've been these years. How my life has been full of trouble. And nobody even cares. Surely, You don't care either. 'Cause, I know there is no God. But if You do exist, please help me know it."

She continued, venting her anger and frustration, until she began to sob... and sob.

"I don't know why I'm crying like this," she wailed. "I... I'm not emotional, but..." Several minutes passed before she regained her composure.

"You know... something has touched me," she whispered. "God, is this You? Making...Yourself known to me? I don't deserve such goodness. Not after the way I have ignored You and treated You."

Before the afternoon was over, she had not only *"touched God,"* but also she had come to appreciate the One who became her Substitute for the guilty debt of sin she could not pay. How wonderfully the Lord chose to manifest Himself to *her*! And to *me*! Indeed, Jesus truly is the Friend of sinners who comes to help them even *before* they want Him.

FATHER, it is a joy to work in a partnership with You. I now have a new confidence in approaching difficult people. I recognize since the "Holy Spirit has fallen upon all flesh," we have a ripe harvest waiting for reapers. Help others to become as excited as I am, in bringing souls into Your family. Amen!

I Don't Want to Repent

WATCHMAN NEE WRITES:
There are many practical difficulties which face the sinner. For example, in the Scriptures we are often told to believe. The Word lays much stress on the necessity of faith. But some folk will insist: 'I have no faith.'

"A girl once said to me—'I can't believe. I would like to believe. But it's no good. I haven't got it in me. The desire's there, but I can't find any faith in me. It's impossible for me to believe.'

"That's alright," I said. "Of course, you can't believe. But you can ask the Lord to give you faith. He is prepared to help you to that extent. You need only to pray—'Lord! Help my unbelief!'"

"Or, the Word tells us that we are to repent. What if we have no desire whatever to repent? I met a student once who said it was too early for him to come to the Lord. He wanted more time in which to taste the pleasures of sin and to enjoy himself.

"The thief on the cross,' He said to me, 'was saved at the last hour. And he had his fling. He waited until he had the last chance to repent. But me...? I... I am still young.'

"Well, what do you want to do?" I asked him.

"I want to wait for another forty years. Have a good time. And then I will repent." So I said to him, "Let us pray."

"Oh, I can't pray," he answered.

"Yes, you can," I said. "You can tell the Lord everything you have told me. He's the *Friend* of unrepentant sinners, like you."

"Oh, I couldn't say that to Him."

"Why not?" I asked.

"Oh, but I could not."

"Well, just be very honest. Whatever is in your heart, you can tell it to Him. He *will* help you!" After Watchman Nee had finished his prayer, he did pray: He told the Lord everything. He said that he did not want to repent. That he wasn't ready to be saved. But that he knew he needed a Savior. At last, he broke down and cried his heart out to Him for help. Meanwhile, the Lord was working repentance in him. He got up from his knees a saved man."

FATHER, I get excited when I discover how You became a friend to help those who are so confused. You have set the pattern, I will follow!

His Polished Boots Did It

AS A BOY. . .
I can still recall two of my father's favorite illustrations. He often used these in Sunday's sermons in churches where he spoke throughout Eastern South Dakota. My dad enjoyed explaining how a merciful act brought a big sergeant to Christ. Once a wicked soldier in a Highland regiment, he became a truly shining witness in the army. The sergeant explained his conversion thus:

"There was a young private in our company who was converted in Malta before our regiment came to Egypt. I am ashamed to admit it, but I, along with other men, gave this fellow an awful time. The Devil seemed to have control over me, and I made that young man's life almost unbearable.

"Well, one terribly wet night, this private came in from sentry duty. He was very tired and very wet. Yet before getting into bed, he knelt down to pray. I took my boots which were heavy with mud, and let the private have it on one side of his head, and then on the other side. He made no response, but continued praying.

"The next morning I found my boots, beautifully polished, sitting by the side of my bed. That was his only reply! His gesture so broke my hard heart, that I was saved that very day. It was the first time I had ever seen a man demonstrating his faith like a true soldier of Our Great Captain. Such love really conquered my hard heart!"

In another story, my dad told of a man who was brought into court for trial and found guilty. It so happened that the judge was a close boyhood friend of the accused, although they had not seen each other for many years. Remaining impartial, the judge sentenced the man and levied a penalty appropriate to his crime. It was a fine so large that the accused could not pay it. A jail sentence, therefore, seemed to be the alternative. Then the judge did a most unusual thing. Leaving the bench, he came down and approached the convicted man. Looking tenderly into his eyes, he shook his hand and then announced, "I'm paying this fine for you."

LORD, I want to thank You for the mercy demonstrated by this young private, and by this judge. Today I also choose to become a demonstrator of Your mercy!

He Took My Place

AN UNGODLY SEA CAPTAIN. . .
lay in his cabin in mid-ocean, death staring him in the face. The dread of eternity weighed heavily upon him.

Captain Coutts sent for his first mate and said, "Williams, get down on your knees and pray for me. I have been very wicked, as you know, and I expect I shall go this time."

"I am not a praying man, you know, captain, so I can't pray. I would if I could."

"Well then, bring a Bible and read me a bit, for my rope is about to run out."

"I have no Bible, captain; you know I'm not a religious man."

"Then send for Thomas, the second mate, to pray for me."

When the second mate came into the presence of his dying captain, he said to him: "I say, Thomas, I am afraid I am bound for eternity this trip. Get down and pray for me. Ask God to have mercy upon my poor soul."

"I'd gladly do it to oblige you, captain, if I could; but I have not prayed since I was a lad."

"Have you a Bible, then, to read to me?"

"No. captain, I have no Bible."

How awful his condition, facing eternity, and without Christ!

They searched the ship over for a man who could pray, but they searched in vain; and for a Bible, but none could be found, until one of the sailors told the captain he had seen a book that looked like a Bible in the hands of the cook's boy, a little fellow named Willie.

"Send at once," said captain Coutts, "and see if he has a Bible." The sailor hurried off to the boy and said to him, "Sonny, have you a Bible?"

"Yes, sir, but I only read it in my own time."

"Oh, that is all right, my lad; take the Bible and go to the captain's cabin. He is sick and wants a Bible. He thinks he is going to die." Away went Willie Platt with his Bible to the captain's cabin.

"Have you a Bible, my boy?"

"Yes, captain."

"Then sit down, and find something in it that will help me, for I am afraid I am going to die. Find something about God having mercy on a sinner like me, and read it to me."

Poor Willie! He did not know where to read, but he remembered that his mother once had him read the 53rd chapter of Isaiah just before he left home.

Willie turned to read that chapter that so fully sets forth the love and mercy of the Lord Jesus Christ in dying for poor sinners such as John Coutts. When Willie got to the fifth verse—*"He was wounded for our transgressions, He was bruised for our iniquities: the chastisement of our peace was upon Him; and with His stripes we are healed,"* the captain interrupted, "Stop, my lad! That sounds like it! Read it again."

Once more Willie read over those blessed words.

"Aye, my lad, that's good—that's it, sure."

These words from the captain encouraged Willie, and he said, "Captain, when I was reading that verse at home, mother made me put my name in it. May I put it in now just where mother told me?"

"Certainly, sonny; put your name in just where your mother told you, and read it again."

Reverently and slowly Willie read the verse:

"He [Jesus] *was wounded for Willie Platt's transgressions, He was bruised for* [Willie Platt's] *iniquities: the chastisement of* [Willie Platt's] *peace was upon Him; and with His stripes* [Willie Platt] *is healed."*

When Willie had finished, the captain was half way over the side of his bed, reaching toward the lad. "Now, my boy, put your captain's name in the verse and read it again—John Coutts, put John Coutts name in there."

Then he slowly read the verse again: *"He* [Jesus] *was wounded for* [John Coutts'] *transgressions, He was bruised for* [John Coutts'] *iniquities: the chastisement of* [John Coutts'] *peace was upon Him; and with His stripes* [John Coutts] *is healed."*

When Willie had finished, the captain said, "That will do, my lad; you may go now."

The captain lay back upon his pillow and repeated over and over again those words of Isaiah 53:5, putting in his own name each time, and as he did so, the joy of heaven filled his soul.

Was he saved? Of course he was saved! Another poor sinner for whom Christ died *"had received Him"* (John 1:12).

What a promise, *"...if thou shalt confess with thy mouth the Lord Jesus, and shalt believe in thine heart that God hath raised Him from the dead, thou shalt be saved"* (Romans 10:9).

Before John Coutts fell asleep in Jesus he had witnessed to everyone on his vessel that Jesus, the Man of Calvary, was wounded for his transgressions, bruised for his iniquities, that the chastisement that he rightfully deserved had fallen on his blessed Substitute.

FATHER, what always amazes me, is that You have someone available to meet every poor sinner's need, at just the right time. It is such a demonstration of Your sovereign hand moving among men—not willing that any should perish! Would You help me not only to be available, but to know how to apply Your word in every crisis time.

The Finger That Pointed

BECAUSE THE SNOW was falling as young Charles Spurgeon made his way to church, he stopped in at a little chapel instead. Only a few people were present because of the storm. When the minister did not arrive, a man from the audience stood to his feet to share an exhortation. Opening his Bible, he began with this verse: *"Look unto Me and be ye saved, all the ends of the earth."*

"My dear friends," he continued, "it's no trouble to *'look.'* You don't have to lift your foot or your finger. You just look. You do not look at yourselves. You look at the Lord Jesus. He is the One who says, *'Look unto Me.'* Do you not see Him hanging on the Cross and dying for you? He says, *'Look unto Me.'* O poor sinner, look unto Him!"

When the man had talked about ten minutes, he suddenly pointed his finger at Charles. "Young man," he said, "you look very miserable. You will always be miserable unless you obey my text. But if you will look in faith to the Lord Jesus this minute, you will be saved!"

That was indeed God's special word! Charles Spurgeon obeyed the invitation. In faith he looked to Jesus and was saved that very moment. Afterward, the young man, who became a mighty prince among preachers in England, enjoyed explaining his experience— "I looked at Him, and He looked at me, and we became one forever!"

One night, Dr. Hall was preaching to a large assembly. He suddenly pointed his finger toward the door, where he saw many standing. "Perhaps, among those pressing in at the door," he spoke directly, "there may be one who is so miserable as to think of throwing himself over yonder bridge. Your load of sin is heavy. Your heart is burdened. You see no way of escape. You may even say to me, 'But, Dr. Hall, it is too late to talk to me, for I am without hope.' But I say to you, Stop! Stop! There is hope for you. There is mercy for you. Christ died for you! He will forgive you. He will save you from the bondage of your sin. Trust Him right now as Your Savior."

Dr. Hall did not know until a few weeks later that at that very moment, just inside the door stood a woman who had made up her mind to throw herself over the bridge. She had stepped into the church to wait until darkness came so the police could not see her and stop her.

As she stood there, she heard Dr. Hall's words and his finger directed toward her. Indeed it was God's special word to her heart. Instead of going to the bridge and ending her life, she came to Christ that night and became a truly happy Christian.

Have you ever sat in an audience and felt the finger of God point to you and uncover your very need? Could it be—at this very moment God's finger is lovingly pointing out something that needs to be changed in your life?

But if I with the finger of God cast out devils, no doubt the kingdom of God is come unto you." (Lk. 11:20)

Then the magicians said unto Pharaoh, This is the finger of God: and Pharaoh's heart was hardened, and he hearkened not unto them as the Lord had said." (Ex. 8:19)

FATHER, it is heartening to know that You are concerned for bringing us to Yourself, but also to full stature in Christ. Let no one be offended. Your Finger is always at work... pointing... pointing to things in our life that need to be changed. We should be thankful that as a loving Father, You will not leave us in our immaturity. Amen!

Divine Harmony

FOR SEVERAL MONTHS. . .
I had been looking forward to participating in the wedding of our niece. To all of us, Lynn and Brett surely represented the Lord's choice for each other. After graduating from Taylor University each had pursued the calling of their preparation for a while. Now they were asking me to "tie the knot." I was delighted to participate.

As with each wedding in the past, I began to ask the Lord for some special word for them. What would distinctly mark God's purpose in bringing their two lives together that they might more effectively fulfill His purpose for them?

Early one morning while reading the Psalms, I came to this verse: *"Mercy and truth are met together..."* (Ps. 85:10) While I was not at that moment consciously looking, that verse struck a note. Yes, that would describe both Brett and Lynn. To all of us who knew Brett, he personified mercy, and to all of us Lynn represented truth. We were already convinced their lives would complement one another.

Now I had a verse to describe them. In all his compassion and caring, Brett (mercy) was vulnerable alone. He needed Lynn to come along side with **truth** to balance and make them complete. To know my niece, Lynn, is to recognize one who is very convinced when a Biblical principle is right; it must be carefully adhered to–even if it has consequences you might not like. Yet sometimes Lynn might "seem" cold, or even harsh in her insistence that "truth is right." So, we concluded God could accomplish in their family a divine balance.

Then as I read further, I realized how *the next line reinforced the same: "righteousness and peace have kissed each other."* I felt it was evident God was bringing Lynn (righteousness) to balance out Brett (peace). Now peace at any price is never right. But being right without any sensitivity for others will not produce harmony. So righteousness and peace need to **kiss each other**. I felt that was an ideal wedding text, don't you agree.

Now to complete the ceremony I needed to add: faith and works got married. Of course this line is not recorded in Psalm 85, but it is written in the small print everywhere in God's Word.

Look at the patriarch Abraham, who surely represents **Faith** throughout the Scriptures. And it seems as though his wife, Sarah, pictures the balancing side: **Works**. Consider how Sarah must have suffered when she heard her husband, Abe, speak of the vast family God had promised them. Yes, her husband Abe could believe their children would number as the stars of the sky, but barren Sarah questioned his wisdom, perhaps even questioned God. Sarah considered their age! They still had no children—not even one.

Sarah could take her husband's impractical (faith) just so long. It was time to (work) help God get this family started. You remember how Sarah suggested a works program which resulted in the birth of a son, Ishmael. It is likely Abe had recognized that Sarah was God's gift to him, and maybe... just maybe her suggestion was right!

So, they agreed to help God! Yes, they did! We now know it was not ordained by God: their fleshly works without true faith produced a tragedy that all history condemns to this day as unfortunate.

"But God... is rich in mercy!"

We remember how God intervened and enabled Abraham and Sarah to bring forth Isaac, a son, who indeed was the fruit of unfeigned Faith and good Works—the blessed fruit of a marriage harmony.

Oh yes, I must finish our story. Almost 20 years have passed. since the wedding. Lynn and Brett enjoy a most blessed marriage that is very fruitful. Four lovely children are discovering the blessing of a balanced, God-centered home.

God's Word continues to remind us:

"Mercy and truth have met,

"Peace and righteousness have kissed..."

Faith (unfeigned) and (good) works got married,

Their children have lived on happily ever since.

FATHER, I see it written in the fabric of things. You have not only made us dependent upon Yourself but dependent upon one another. Each of us is not only different from the other, but in a sense we are incomplete. Unless You dwell within us we will compete instead of complete.. It is such a joy to know: all things are designed according to Your Divine purpose.

In order to make any progress in our journey we are seeing how God has designed that no single quality can stand alone. As each virtue bows before Him, the Maker of all virtues, He can work out a blessed harmony. Brett must lay down his insistence that mercy alone is right; and Lynn must lay down her insistence that truth alone is right.

As each is willing to give up their right to be right, God brings forth HIS OWN WILL... and harmony is born.

Different by Design

I'm sure you have considered what I choose to call the DDD factor. Though I have recognized that this factor did exist for many years, I have only recently used this title to explain

...why in marriage opposites attract—(such as mercy and truth).

...why in theology both sovereignty and responsibility exist.

...why every church has Marthas (do-ers) and Marys (be-ers).

...why in every church you have both "catchers" and "menders."

...why in elders meetings you have inclusives and exclusives.

...why in prayer meeting you have the silent (listeners to God) and the vocal (talkers to God.)

...why in every family you have the cautious and the decisive.

...why in every family you have both the receivers and givers.

...why in every church fellowship you have passive (quietists who wait,) and you have active (pietists who move).

...why in every country you have both settlers and pioneers.

It becomes evident in every arena of life that we have people who act differently. Did this just happen, or should we recognize this as a **Deliberately Designed Difference** (or limitation)? The more I see this factor, which seems to be built-into the fabric of things, I conclude it is God's way of bringing balance—His way of showing our need for one another, but also our great need for Him.

To express it still another way, let us describe this as God's **Divinely-Determined-Dependency**. From the very beginning God has determined to keep all moral functions dependent upon Him, i.e. in His control continually!

Man's treacherous (immoral) act of independence, which is his insistence upon "doing it without God," continues to increase until the final harvest comes. But thank God, He is now raising up a kingdom of saints who gladly embrace this way of dependency. They see it not as limitation but as the way of greater fulfillment. To them, God is not only the Creator but He remains the Sustainer of all things: "For of Him, and through Him and to Him are all things..."

Thus far in our stories we have recognized how mercy and truth are like two wings of a bird; how peace and righteousness also need to complete one another. Yet too often these very virtues become <u>competing</u> issues, when God has designed them to be <u>completing</u> issues. Competing or completing–which will it be? How can mercy and truth complete one another, and accomplish God's intention? I'll try to explain it this way: if truth (is a thesis) and mercy (is an antithesis)–and only as both die, can they come into synthesis(or resurrection), then a new agreement or divine harmony is possible. God's order and arrangement reveals wisdom. Let us not try to improve on His ways.

We must emphasize again, that if we try to keep this universe principles-centered we will remain frustrated, for every principle has its counter-balancing principle. God Himself must choose: will it be mercy or truth? will it be peace or righteousness? Or will it be both? Because we are forever dependent upon a word (rhema) from the Lord, it is imperative that we recognize...

this universe is Person-centered, but
by His design it is principles-governed,
and will be purpose fulfilling.

FATHER, I know this lesson may seem very philosophical and be difficult for some. Grant us Your very special help. I pray right now that You will enlighten minds to recognize the importance of allowing "the cross to work" a death blow to our natural reasonings. Only as we are wholly dependent upon You, will "Your light" break in, and we shall TRUST Your direction. The Apostle Paul describes it in these verses in Romans:

O the depth of the riches both of the wisdom and knowledge of God! How unsearchable are His judgments, and his ways past finding out! For who hath known the mind of the Lord? Or who hath been His counselor? O who hath first given to Him, and it shall be recompensed unto Him again? For of Him and through Him, and to Him, are all things: to whom be glory for ever. Amen

Challenging the System

ONE DAY DURING HIS PRAYER time, the monk, Telemachus received the inner sense that God wanted him to go to Rome. Of course he was excited in visiting Rome at this time for she was then celebrating her victory over the Gauls.

The Colosseum, filled with fifty thousand people, watched the festivities as gladiators fought each other and wild beasts in the center of the Colosseum. The crowds were ecstatic with excitement, but it was most painful for Telemachus to watch the bloodshed of men and animals. In that hour he realized why God had led him to Rome. He was hearing... and he must obey!

A fire kindled in his spirit and he could no longer watch this slaughter of life as thousands cheered. He must! He would! He ran down the aisle and jumped over the railing into the arena. Suddenly the crowd grew silent. They had never seen a spectator jump into the arena with the wild beasts and gladiators.

Standing in their midst, Telemachus shouted, "In the Name of Jesus Christ, stop!" The people in the stands thought he was just a crazy old man. One of the gladiators took the flat side of his sword and slapped him in the face. He fell, got up and again cried out, "In the name of Jesus Christ, stop!" It seemed to ignite the frenzy of the crowd, and someone shouted, "Kill him." The gladiator obliged. Telemachus fell to the ground and died.

Stunned by this awful ordeal, the crowd began leaving the Colosseum until it was empty. Amazing! That moment of bravery ushered in a change. The bloody games in the Colosseum stopped from that time on. Mercy was crying out: no more slaughter of life. Truth was exposing the foolishness of such insane pleasure. Whether he was at that moment led by God is not the issue. One man was willing to challenge the social system. When mercy and truth meet—there is a compelling announcement to all.

A professor was asked one day about the biblical approach to social justice. He suggested that our social concern should include:

(1) Alms giving—which is immediate relief. For example, giving a person a fish so he or she can eat today (our daily bread).

(2) Development—teaching a person to fish, so he has the skills and tools to earn his own way. For example, instruction in digging wells, providing tools or teaching technology.

(3) Structural change—concerns how to get the person a share of the fish ponds, so he or she has access to fishing for a lifetime. This can include owning land or access to an education. Structural change often involves challenging corruption in politics or religion.

Now we face the battle of this century. Some insist that the biblical, evangelical way is CONFRONTATION. There are a lot of reasons why people are poor. Some are poor because they are lazy and without any hope. Some are poor because they hold a world view that ignores God. Hinduism is a good example of a society that is poor because of a wrong God-concept. Many insist that only by confronting the darkness with truth and bringing folk into a personal relationship with Jesus Christ can we hope for any real lasting change.

There are others who insist that modeling a "BETTER LIFE-STYLE" will entice folk to change their ways. When we demonstrate the fruit of the gospel, we help them recognize they are bankrupt; that only a change on the inside can bring any radical change of character. They must first see it in our manner of life. There is no question that Telemachus shocked Rome and her evil social structure. Until we embrace the root of the gospel, social structures will never change.

Of course the core of sin is our essential rebellion against God. We want to keep self rather than God at the center of our universe! That results in all kinds of selfishness. No amount of good social activity will fundamentally change that basic self-centeredness. The root of the gospel is bringing a person to Christ, who lays the axe to that selfish core. Only then does any person become merciful toward others and truth changes his attitude toward life.

Our challenge! Accept no half measures. Mercy without truth will only produce sentimentality. Truth without mercy will only produce an empty, mechanical action—void of a compassionate heart.

FATHER, How can I keep both mercy and truth in balance? You are directing me back to our primary issue: When I am diligently listening for Your voice and determined to obey, I can TRUST that You will either confront with truth, or You will continue to demonstrate a Godly "life-style" through me. I am available!

The Prison Clock Strikes

J. SIDLOW BAXTER

explains: I have known some anti-supernaturalists who were won over to the Christian faith through the impressive evidence of divine guidance in the lives of believers. Some of these skeptics had been students of philosophy and psychology, and were pretty brainwashed in the modern distrust of subjective experience. They could (at least to their own satisfaction) scientifically analyze away any such "experience."

Yet now these same persons are convinced believers, knowing that they are dealing with a reality which simply cannot be satisfactorily accounted for by purely natural or human forces. That which argument could never prove to them, experience has demonstrated. Let me offer this illustration to prove my point:

One morning, while a minister friend of mine was busy in his study, his mind was suddenly gripped by a strong conviction that he should visit a certain jail to see a man who was under death sentence for murder. He did not know the condemned man, but he knew some of the circumstances of the crime.

The condemned man had been a decent-living fellow, and apparently comfortably married, except that his wife had begun to drink and eventually a wrong relationship had developed with another man. This was brought to the notice of her husband who waylaid the other man with only the intent to thrash him. Instead, he murdered him.

The jail was a train journey away. Even if the minister went there, he wondered if he would be allowed to see the man. Besides, what good could it do now? Yet he had been praying earlier that the day might be guided, and he was convinced now that the strange urge was really from the Holy Spirit.

After finding a suitable train, he decided to go. As 'the stars in their courses fought against Sisera,' so it seemed everything was set on preventing his getting that train, but he got it 'in the nick of time,' and eventually reached the prison.

After the usual formalities he was admitted. Then for some reason there was delay due to hesitation by the prison authorities. Finally, he received permission to see the condemned man. At the cell only a small grating was opened and he stood face to face with the prisoner. He began quickly to explain the seemingly strange reason for his coming and how he would have arrived earlier but for delays. Just then, the boom of the prison clock reverberated through the corridor as it slowly struck two o'clock in the afternoon.

As the sound died away, the prisoner suddenly burst into convulsive sobbing. Struggling to control himself, he groaned out the words, "I never meant to kill...but...I am to die. This morning, in my agony, I cried, Oh! God, if You really exist and if You really hear, and if You care, please, oh please, let me know in some way...and,... God, I give You until two o'clock this afternoon!"

When my minister friend left the prison a bit later, the young man in that cell had truly found the glad assurance of eternal salvation in Christ. My friend went home gratefully musing on the wonderful guidance which had contrived his arrival at that prison cell just as the prison clock boomed out two o'clock!"

If guidance gives to life a sense of mission and the sense of accountability every moment, then we can see the importance of expecting God to help us develop greater sensitivity to His inner prompting. However, it would seem the great problem for God is how to guide us and not override us. He must both guide us and develop us as persons at the same time: to lead us and at the same time produce initiative in us is a task worthy of divine wisdom.

J. SIDLOW BAXTER shares another example: "One Sunday morning just as my dear wife was entering her usual pew at the church, she became strangely but irresistibly constrained to sit near the front with a certain lady who at that time was beset by sore trial. Momentarily she hesitated lest her unusual action should give a wrong impression to those around or cause embarrassment to the lady herself. Yet along with the surprise urge came a peaceful assurance that it was of the Spirit; so she acted accordingly.

It was not until many months later that she learned what this bit of obeyed guidance had meant. The saintly woman with whom my wife went to sit had been struggling with the problem as to whether she should still come to church, owing to the ugly scandal now associated with the family name. Because she was scared of curious looks and questions, she had pleaded:

"Dear Lord, guide me! Preserve me from unwise inquirers; and, if it please Thee, give me a sign—may Mrs Baxter be led to come and sit with me."

Seven Singing Soldiers

WE HAVE BEEN CONSIDERING. . .
how God delights to work in situations that seem impossible. This
story comes from the Finnish-Russian War. Seven soldiers of the Red
Army had been captured by the Finnish soldiers and were waiting
their execution in the morning. One of the officers in General
Amnerheim's army explains how this small town had been under
siege—first captured by the Reds and then retaken by the Finns. A
Finnish officer relates how the Red prisoners under his guard acted
during that long Sunday night before they were to be shot on
Monday morning.

Seven prisoners were kept in the basement of the Town Hall. In
the passageway my men stood at attention with their rifles. The
atmosphere was filled with hatred. My soldiers were drunk with success and taunted their prisoners, who swore and beat on the walls
with their bleeding fists. Many called for their wives and children
who were far away. At dawn they were all to die.

It was true enough that we had won the victory, but the value of
this seemed to diminish as the night advanced, and something
strange happened. One of the men doomed to death began to sing.
"He is mad," was everybody's first thought, but I had noticed that this
man, Koskinen, had not raved and cursed. Quietly he sat on his
bench, a picture of utter despair. Nobody said anything. Each was
carrying his own burden in his own way. Koskinen began to sing—
a bit wavering at first. Then his voice grew stronger, becoming natural and free. All the prisoners turned and looked at him as he
sang—

"Safe in the arms of Jesus, Safe on His gentle breast,
There by His love o'ershaded, Sweetly my soul shall rest.
Hark, it's the voice of angels, Borne in a song to me,
Over the fields of jasper, Over the crystal sea."

Over and over again he sang that verse. When he finished everyone was quiet for a few minutes until a wild looking man broke out—
"Where did you get that, you fool? Are you trying to make us
religious?"

Koskinen looked at his comrades with tear-filled eyes.

"Comrade," he said quietly. "Will you listen to me for a minute?
You asked me where I got this song. It was from the Salvation Army.
I heard it three weeks ago. My mother sang about Jesus and prayed
to Him."

He stopped for a little while, as if to gather strength. Then, he rose to his feet. Being the soldier that he was, he looked straight in front of him aÜnd contin ued.

"It is cowardly to hide your beliefs. The God my mother believed in is now my God. I cannot tell how it happened. I lay a ake last night, and suddenly saw Mother's face before me. It reminded me of the song that I had heard. I felt I had to find the Savior and hide in Him. Then I prayed like the thief on the cross, that Christ would forgive me and cleanse my sinful soul and make me ready to stand before the One I should soon meet.

"It was a strange night," Koskinen continued. "There were times when everything seemed to shine around me. Verses from the Bible and from the Song Book came to my mind. They brought messages of the crucified Savior, the Blood that cleanses from sin, and the Home He has prepared for us. I thanked Him. I accepted Him. And since then, this song has been sounding inside me. It was God's answer to my prayer. I could no longer keep it to myself. Within a few hours, I shall be with the Lord—saved by His grace."

Koskinen's face shone as if by an inward light. His comrades sat there quietly, yet he stood there transfixed. Every one of my soldiers was listening to what this Red Revolutionary had to say.

"You are right, Koskinen," said one of his comrades at last. "If only I knew there was mercy for me too. These hands of mine have shed blood. I have reviled God and trampled on all that is holy. Now I realize there is a hell, and it is the proper place for me."

As he sank to the floor with despair on his face, he groaned, "Pray for me. Tomorrow I shall die, and my soul will be in the hands of the Devil!"

Next, two Red soldiers went down on their knees and prayed for each other. It was no long prayer, but it reached Heaven. We who listened to it forgot our hatred. It melted in the light of Heaven, for here were two men who were soon to die, seeking reconciliation with their God.

Let me tell you that by the time it was four o'clock, all Koskinen's comrades had followed his example and began to pray. The change in the atmosphere was indescribable. Some of the seven sat on the floor. Some on the benches. Some wept quietly. Others talked of spiritual things. None of us had a Bible, but the Spirit of God spoke to us all. Then someone remembered those at home, and there followed an hour of intense letter writing. Confessions and tears were in those letters. The night had almost gone, and the day was dawning. No one had a moment of sleep.

"Sing the song once more for us, Koskinen," said one of them. You should have heard them sing, not only that song, but other verses and choruses long forgotten. Soon the soldiers on guard united with them. The power of God had touched all. And everything had changed. The venerable basement of Town Hall resounded in that early morning hour with the songs of the Blood of the Lamb.

The clock struck six. How I wished I could have begged mercy for these men, but I knew that was impossible. Between two rows of soldiers they marched out to the place of execution. One of them asked to be allowed to sing Koskinen's song once again, and permission was granted. Then they asked to be allowed to die with uncovered faces. With hands lifted to Heaven, they sang one last time with might and main, **"Safe in the arms of Jesus."**

When the last line had died out, the lieutenant gave the word, "fire!" Seven Red soldiers who had fought their last fight, went to meet their Maker. We inclined our heads in silent prayer.

What happened in the hearts of the other guards I do not know, but as far as I am concerned, I was a new man from that hour. I had met Christ in one of His lowliest and youngest disciples. I had seen enough to realize that I too could be His.

Is any heart too hard for the Lord? God's grace and mercy had conquered both the prisoners and the guards during that unforgettable night. It was the "Spirit poured out on all flesh," that all who were wholly honest toward God might "touch" the Friend of Sinners and find eternal salvation.

Finally, we need to remember that God rejoices, and we also rejoice over every one who comes to Him in repentance. However, there is both joy and sadness. These seven men who were rescued from hell and who received eternal life had never run life's race. While they experienced God's grace that night, they had never fulfilled His purpose—they had nothing to offer God.

FATHER, this is a most sobering thought. I am thankful I have learned about living to fulfill Your purpose. As we have said before, purpose and grace should not be separated. However, there are times, as with these seven soldiers, when grace comes to men and they have no opportunity for running life's race to fulfill God's purpose. Surely to reach heaven is most wonderful. Yet it is tragic when You get nothing from our life-time. Perhaps (dear reader), you would like to join me in asking God's special help. For we don't want to just reach heaven, we want to receive Your smile of approval when we get there. Amen!

Her Story Lives On

THE PRISONERS in the Montinlupa Prison who gathered for a large assembly were astonished to see a woman in her seventies make her way up the steps of the platform to address them. They wondered what this old woman would have to say to them?

With much difficulty she explained how she and her family had hidden Jews from the Nazi during World War II; how German police, because of a tip from two of her fellow citizens, had pounded on their door one frigid February day in 1944 with warrants for their arrest. The speaker was Corrie ten Boom... survivor!

After the war was over, the two fellow Dutchmen who had betrayed her family were taken into custody and put on trial... "My sister Nollie," Corrie told her audience," heard of the trial of these two men who told the Gestapo about us, and she wrote a letter to both of them. She explained that we had forgiven them; that we could do this because of the Lord Jesus, and His mercy."

Both men responded. One wrote "I have received Jesus as my Savior. When God can give such ability to forgive to people like Corrie ten Boom and her sister, then there is hope for me. I brought my sins to Him (and He forgave me)."

The other letter received an opposite response: "I know what I have done to your family, that I have caused the death of several of you who have saved Jews, and above that I have helped to kill many hundreds of Jewish people. The only thing I regret is that I have not been able to kill more of your kind."

The Holy Spirit brought a hush over that crowd as Corrie went on to challenge the prisoners. Each of them—even as the criminals who had been on either side of Jesus on the Cross—had a choice to make. Each one could accept or reject Christ and His forgiveness.

One of those criminals who rejected—shouted insults at Jesus: "Aren't you the Christ? Then save yourself and us." But the other criminal stopped him and said, "You should fear God! We are punished justly, getting what we deserve for what we did. But this man has done nothing wrong."

FATHER, I love the merciful response Jesus made to this criminal: "I tell you the truth, today you will be with me in paradise."

Who Are You Following?

IT IS UNWISE TO ACCEPT. . . the leadership of anyone whose character is unknown. Very many undiscerning people have suffered from placing themselves under the guidance of a leader, who presented an enticing story and promised great gain. Congressman Hobson used this humorous incident to warn folk that they should not expect this unusual deliverance when accepting leadership from someone they do not know.

Mrs. Exe stood on a crowded corner, when the traffic was at its height, staring at the thickly tangled come-and-go of cars and cabs, and not daring to venture in among the dangers of that moving mass.

"May I cross the street with you, madam?" She turned, and saw an elderly stranger with lifted hat and gallant smile.

"Oh, thank you," said Mrs. Exe, and the stranger grasped her arm with a firm grip, and together they plunged boldly into the wild crush of moving vehicles.

In and out, right and left, up and down, they zigzagged, at imminent peril of life and limb. Pedestrians on the sidewalk stopped and looked at them. Drivers and chauffeurs shouted and swore at them. It was plain to all that they were in unusual danger. The escort of Mrs. Exe, still wearing his gallant smile, still grasping her arm, really seemed to make no effort to avoid the oncoming vehicles. He darted erratically, and yet calmly, this way and that.

At last, by a miracle, the other side was reached. Mrs. Exe then jerked her arm away from her escort's grasp. "It's no thanks to you," she said, with a look of scorn, "that we weren't both killed. Why, the way you positively courted danger, I would think you were blind!"

"Madam, I am blind," he replied. "That's why I asked if I could cross the street with you."

What is so very tragic is that many who are spiritually blind do not even realize how blind they are. But that is not the point of our choosing this incident. Both Mrs Exe and the blind man had their own misplaced expectations. That is usually our first mistake.

Every year thousands of pastors are leaving the pulpit for various reasons. Often this could be remedied by simply understanding that everyone has misplaced expectations. What should a pastor expect from his flock? What should members expect from a pastor?

All leaders need the encouragement that you are asking God to give them His direction. It is not appropriate to point a finger and insist we are expecting you to find God's way for us. The "you and us" needs to go. When leaders know you are praying with them and "together we are asking God for His leadership," it brings a new measure of confidence. Every true leader I know will acknowledge that God alone can guide His flock to new levels in their spiritual journey.

So, leaders, be quick to impart this lowly spirit in which you lead. Never allow the "you and I" to dominate, but rather "we together" must learn to pray through this crisis for God's direction.

A.W. Tozer advises: "In any group of ten persons at least nine are sure to believe that they are qualified to offer advice to others. And in no field of human interest are people as ready to offer advice as in the field of religion and morals. Yet it is precisely in this field that the average person is least qualified to speak wisely and is capable of the most harm when he does speak. For this reason we should select our counselors carefully..."

God's way is to acknowledge that "we must together seek His face for direction". And we must learn to wait before Him, until His way becomes clear to those who have an ear to hear.

Tozer continues: "Before we follow any man we should look for the oil on his forehead. We are under no spiritual obligation to aid any man in any activity that has not upon it the marks of the cross. No appeal to our sympathies, no sad stories, no shocking pictures should move us to put our money and our time into schemes promoted by persons who are too busy to listen to God."

What is our answer to those who too quickly accept the opinions of others and adopt them as their own? Those who boast the loudest of their independence—as though that were a virtue—need to bring their individualistic spirit to the cross. If they truly have "a word from the Lord," God will confirm that through the group who listen to God.

Father, the more I know You, I recognize You are longsuffering in adjusting all our expectations. Surely, You are the Father of all mercies:

It is of the Lord's mercies that we are not consumed, because his compassions fail not. They are new every morning: great is Thy faithfulness. (Lam. 3:22-23).

Looking For a Platform

FROM THE PEOPLE'S REPUBLIC. . . of China comes this story of Pastor John, a servant responsible for distributing a large number of Bibles he had hidden in a barn. Before he could finish his work he was arrested. Interrogators attempted to break him through prolonged torture, however, they didn't know what to do with a man who was not afraid to die.

Pastor John was taken by the police into the courtyard of the prison and forced to stand upright on a tall, wooden box. The box was about four feet high and very narrow. In fact, there was just room for his two feet on top of the box.

Then the police put a noose around his neck, tightened it, and fixed it to a crossed wooden beam just above his head.

"We have given up on you," his interrogators shouted at him. "The moment you move or your legs collapse, you will hang yourself. This will be your penalty for your stubbornness."

Since they were afraid to kill him, they had determined to let him fall and thus kill himself—and call it suicide.

Two policemen were assigned to watch Pastor John during his last moments—so they thought. Other interrogators watched through a hidden window from a distance.

However, the nearby policemen hardly looked up at Pastor John. Instead, they gambled. (It sounds familiar, doesn't it).

"I felt so weak as they gambled at my feet," Pastor John said, "but I felt a constant surge of strength in my body. I could identify with Jesus Christ on His cross. I do not know! Perhaps He too looked down and felt the same pity, when He saw the soldiers casting lots for His clothes. They were so utterly indifferent to His agonies."

Yet he did experience agonies. Pastor John's body cried out for sleep. His legs began to swell. Day passed into night, and night into yet another day. Pastor John remained still. He didn't move. He started talking to the policemen. He told them about Jesus, and that he wasn't afraid of death because of Jesus.

"Old man," laughed one of the policemen, "when I get to be seventy like you, and look as unhealthy as you do, I won't be afraid to die either." And he burst out laughing again.

Pastor John's legs developed cramps and continued to swell. All feeling was gone. Four days and four nights had gone by. And day five. Then six. Then the seventh day and night. His only relief was the rain. He stuck out his dry, thickened tongue, to gain a few drops of moisture. It also seemed to wash his weary body.

Day eight passed. Also day nine. The word was getting around in prison. It was as though a holy hush gathered over the compound.

"No man can survive that long," they would say. "No food, no water, no rest. This is impossible."

Days ten, eleven, twelve and finally, day thirteen arrived. Now it was time for God to speak. Pastor John still stood on the narrow box, with the noose tight around his neck,... he would not let go.

His legs were swollen—almost beyond description. The policemen continued to look on in wonder Everyone in the prison seemed to be holding their breath as the tension continued.

Suddenly, a huge thunderstorm hit the prison. The sky went black. The rain pelted down. Pastor John's resistance finally reached an end. At a crack of lightening, followed by a crash of thunder, so loud that it shook the prison—Pastor John felt sure it was all over.

In his delirium, vaguely hearing the thunder, he thought he was falling into the arms of Jesus as the noose tightened around his neck.

Then, he awakened. He found himself soaking wet, lying in a small room. Amazing! He was not in the arms of Jesus, but in the arms of two policemen. One of them was splashing water on his face. The other was massaging his legs. All Pastor John could do was to cry in pain.

Both policemen were crying, "Please don't die! Please don't die!"

"Why?" He said. "Why can't I die?"

"Because, we want to know about your Jesus," they replied. At the very moment you fell, a flash of lightning cut the rope just above your head... Please don't tell us that your Jesus didn't save you, we know He did. We know He sent the lightning to cut the noose."

Pastor John was released, and there was no more interrogation.

Later, the Bibles were quietly distributed. Today, they are a great source of comfort to millions of Chinese.

How do we explain this amazing incident? May I suggest that God is always looking for some platform on which He can demonstrate His grace and mercy. Just as He chose Job of old, He now chose Pastor John to be a living example to the whole world, What God will do through one man who becomes available. God chose John and demonstrated great mercy toward John, but also great mercy to his persecutors.

Perhaps the question that confronts us is this: Am I willing to become a platform on which God can demonstrate something of His character?

> *"...showing mercy unto thousands of them that love*
> *Me and keep My commandments."*

FATHER, I must truthfully respond: "I cannot say that I am willing, but I am ready for You to help me become willing."

Pardon For An Enemy

TWO BOYS. . .
went to the same school—George Washington and Peter Miller. Washington became the first president of the United States and Peter Miller became a preacher of the Gospel. Washington lived at Philadelphia, and Miller at Ephrata—a village seventy miles from the capital. For many years preacher Miller endured much persecution from a man named Michael Wittman, who did all he could to distress the servant of God. He even inflicted personal violence, damaged the church building, and denounced publicly the preacher's testimony.

At length Wittman was involved in treason, was arrested, and sentenced to death. Upon hearing this, preacher Miller walked the seventy miles to Philadelphia to see his friend, George Washington, and to plead for the life of his persecutor.

"Well, Peter, what can I do for you?" George asked.

"For our old acquaintance' sake, George, I have come to ask you to pardon the sentence of the traitor, Wittman."

"No, Peter. This case is too black. I cannot give you the life of your friend."

"My *friend!* He is the bitterest enemy any man has ever had." Then he told the president what pain he had suffered from this man for over twenty years.

"Ah, then, Peter; this puts another aspect upon the matter. I could not give you the life of your *friend*; but I will freely pardon your *enemy.*"

Three days later preacher Miller walked with his enemy, Wittman, back the seventy miles to Ephrata. During this walk, Wittman's heart was melted. He questioned why he had been pardoned. Why did Peter Miller care so much for him? Gradually mercy began to dawn on him, as light broke in to his darkened heart. He surrendered himself to God, was converted, and asked Peter, the man who had shown such mercy, to baptize him.

Speak and act as those who are going to be judged by the law that gives freedom, because judgment without mercy will be shown to anyone who has not been merciful. Mercy triumphs over judgment. (NIV James 2:12-13).

FATHER, it always astounds us how You "show mercy to whom You will show mercy." In Your selective mercy You have a reason but it is not known to us now. We are sure there will come a day when we shall understand the mystery of Your mercy. For now, we simply rejoice in Your mercy.

Special Earthquake Mercy

APART FROM GOD'S merciful intervention, how shall we explain what happened to Lisa.

At three o'clock on the morning of September 19, she gave birth to a healthy nine pound baby at the Mexico City Medical Center. Around six o'clock that morning, the nurses came around telling all the new mothers to rise for their baths. Humanly speaking, Lisa felt miserable, but obeyed and received the strength needed.

When she finished, a doctor came up to her.

"Daughter!" he said, "Please follow me."

He started going down the stairs in the opposite direction. But she stopped, telling him that the elevators were going in the other direction.

"I know all about that," he replied. "Just follow me."

Lisa received supernatural strength and walked down three flights of stairs.

"But doctor! My baby!" She called out.

Again, he reassured her, telling her he knew all about that. They continued down the stairs. Then they reached the second floor, where the ward was full of new-born babies.

"But doctor," she said, "how am I going to know which baby is mine?"

"I know which one is yours," the doctor replied.

He went directly to the crib, picked him up, and gave him to his mother. She immediately confirmed his identity by his bracelet. Then the doctor disappeared!

Lisa walked down to the first floor. Suddenly, she whirled around to see the other side of the hospital where she had been— collapsing! It was the morning of the Mexico City earthquake... Sept. 19th.

Among the survivors, Lisa inquired about the doctor, giving them a description of what he looked like. They insisted no one had ever seen a doctor with that description.

Lisa went home that afternoon, and later came to the Christian Center, testifying, with many tears, of God's mercy in sparing her life. Could it be that God had sent an angel to deliver her from destruction. What a monumental experience for a young believer to become established in the mercy and grace of the Lord!

God's special favor delivering Lisa and her baby cannot be explained. Was it because of some special worthiness in her or a purpose to be worked out in her life? There were hundreds in Mexico City who lost their lives that day.

Father, Your mercy remains a mystery to us. You only reply, *"I will have mercy on whom I will have mercy." It is so true we now see through a glass that is darkened. Some day we shall know, even as we are known.* For now, You ask us to simply TRUST You. We do!

Could You Have Loved as Much?

BOB CONSIDINE WRITES. . .

EDITH TAYLOR was sure that she was "the luckiest woman on the block." She and Karl had been married twenty-three years, and her heart still skipped a beat when he walked into the room. As for Karl, he gave every appearance of a man in love with his wife. If his job as a government warehouse worker took him out of town, he would write Edith each night and send gifts from every place he visited.

In February 1950, Karl was sent to Okinawa for a few months to work in a new government warehouse. It was a long time to be away, and so far. This time no little gifts came. Edith understood! He was saving his money for the house they had long dreamed of owning someday.

The lonesome months dragged on. Each time Edith expected Karl home, he'd write that he must stay "another three weeks." "Another month." "Just two months longer." He'd been gone a year now, and his letters were coming less and less often. No gifts ... she understood. But a few pennies for a postage stamp? Then, after weeks of silence, came this letter:

Dear Edith,

I wish there was a kinder way to tell you that we are no longer married.

Edith walked to the sofa and sat down. He had written to Mexico for a mail-order divorce. He had married Aiko, a Japanese maid-of-all-work assigned to his quarters. She was nineteen. Edith was forty-eight.

Now, if I were making up this story, the rejected wife would fight that quick paper-divorce. She would hate her husband and the woman. She would want vengeance for her own shattered life. But I am describing here simply what did happen. Edith Taylor did not hate Karl. Perhaps she had loved him so long that she was unable to stop.

She could picture the situation. A lonely man. Constant closeness. But even so, Karl had done the easy, shameful thing. He had chosen divorce, rather than taking advantage of the young servant girl. The only thing Edith could not believe was that he had stopped loving her. Someday, somehow, Karl would come home.

Edith now built her life around this thought. She wrote Karl, asking him to keep her in touch. In time he wrote that he and Aiko were expecting a baby. Maria was born in 1951; then in 1953, Helen. Edith sent gifts to the little girls. She still wrote to Karl and he wrote back: "Helen had a tooth... Aiko's English was improving... Karl had lost weight."

And then the terrible letter. Karl was dying of lung cancer. His last letters were filled with fear. Not for himself, but for Aiko and his two little girls. He had been saving to send them to school in America, but his hospital bills were taking everything. What would become of them?

Then Edith knew that her last gift to Karl could be peace of mind. She wrote that if Aiko was willing, she would take Maria and Helen and bring them up in Waltham. For many months after Karl's death, Aiko would not let the children go. They were all she had ever known. Yet what could she offer them except a life of poverty, servitude and despair? In November 1956, she sent the two girls to Edith.

Edith had known it would be hard at fifty-four to be mother to a three-year-old and five-year-old. She hadn't realized that, in the time since Karl's death, they would forget the little English they knew. But Maria and Helen learned fast. The fear left their eyes; their faces grew plump. And Edith, for the first time in six years, was hurrying home from work. Even getting meals was fun again! Sadder were the times when letters came from Aiko: "Aunt, tell me...if Maria or Helen cry or not." In the broken English, Edith read the loneliness, and she knew what loneliness was. She knew that she must bring the girls' mother here too.

She must make the decision, but Aiko was still a Japanese citizen, and the immigration quota had a waiting list many years long. It was then that Edith Taylor wrote me, asking if I could help. I described the situation in my newspaper column. Others did more. Petitions were started, and, in August 1957, Aiko Taylor was permitted to enter the country.

As the plane came in at New York's international airport, Edith had a moment of fear. What if she should hate this woman who had taken Karl away from her? The last person off the plane was a girl so thin and small that Edith thought at first she was a child. She stood there clutching the railing, and Edith knew that, if she had been afraid, Aiko was near panic.

She called Aiko's name, and the girl rushed down the steps into Edith's arms. As they held each other, Edith had an extraordinary thought. "I prayed for Karl to come back. Now he has—in his two little daughters and in this gentle girl he loved. Help me, God, to love her, too." (B.C.)

I feel sure many wives would have exhorted Edith:
"Forget him! Get on with your own life."
To some that may seem like sound advice, but that is not what Edith felt God wanted for her, and we appreciate her decision. She might even have questioned in weak moments: "Was it really God telling her to forgive, and forgive some more?" Yes, she chose to send her roots deeper into the river of his grace: And God responded by giving her two daughters and a close friend.

It is awesome! when God writes the last chapter, for whatever He writes is good... good for all. The Psalmist seems to know this:
"I will bless the Lord who hath given me counsel: my reins also instruct me in the night seasons. I have set the Lord always before me: because he is at my right hand, I shall not be moved. Therefore my heart is glad, and my glory rejoiceth: my flesh shall rest in hope...Thou wilt show me the path of life: in thy presence is fullness of joy; at thy right hand there are pleasures for evermore." Let us be assured...
"...weeping may endure for a night,
but joy cometh in the morning!"

FATHER, I am sure that I could not endure as Edith did, but I remember that You are the One Who provides special grace for those Who choose Your best. I now choose to become Your channel for loving all the "Aikos" and their children around me, who are helpless victims of sin and lust.

Extravagant Love

J. DAVID NEWMAN

THE CHURCH members were aghast! Saying "goodbye" to the pastor with flowers was one thing, but *$20,000 worth* of flowers?

This was Pastor Tom Phillips' last sermon in this church. The farewell committee had planned to place several extra-large bouquets in front of the pulpit. But when the committee members arrived at the church, they found that someone had been there before them.

Behold! Flowers filled the entire sanctuary! They flooded the rostrum, hid the sides and back of the sanctuary, and even covered the ends of the pews. And these weren't just common, ordinary flowers. There were rare orchids from the Orient, exotic roses, unique dahlias imported from Mexico—the list was endless. Stepping into the church was like entering a perfumed Shangri-La.

As the members gathered for this farewell service, an incredulous murmuring could be heard.

"You say she spent $20,000 on these flowers—a year's salary?" ... Isn't she the one who seduced a high official in the government, blackmailed him, and then sold state secrets to enemy agents?... Those flowers will be dead in a few days; that money could have been better spent in our inner-city mission."

The pastor's sermon began with a verse: *"Greater love has no one than this, that he lay down his life for his friends"* (Jn. 15:13).

"God worked through me," he continued, "to save Helen from a life of debauchery and hopelessness. Only those of you who have been where she has been can appreciate how she feels now. She could not lay down her life for me to show her gratitude. So she made another great sacrifice. She spent her life's savings on these flowers." (D.J.M)

I wish I had been there to hear the pastor's explanation; I am told he turned their attention to this analogy of Mary's anointing of Jesus' feet with precious ointment from her alabaster box. Many have asked, why did Jesus allow Mary to pour the ointment on His feet?

These two incidents are very different, yet they do illustrate our inmate proclivity to judging and condemning such "seemingly extravagant love". We recall the disciples response to Mary's love gesture. They whispered: "...why this waste... could it not have been used..." Jesus was quick to protect Mary from their vicious tongues. In Him we see how mercy (loving kindness) and truth (reality) meet.

Remember that God's mercy is most meaningful to those who have been most deeply bruised. Mary had been bruised and so had this restored sister. Each were expressing their heart of thanksgiving by this costly sacrifice.

There is one sentence I think we usually misinterpret. Jesus must explain it: "...the bruised reed He will not break." In the Bible times the shepherd played music upon these reeds. They were easily bruised. Because the shepherd could make another, he would snap the old one, throw it away and make a new one.

However, the good news is that Our Shepherd does not throw away any bruised reed. When the music has gone out of a person who has been bruised, with a tender hand of mercy He mends and restores it. So, this phrase becomes more meaningful: "...the bruised reed He will not break..."

With great compassion Pastor Phillips was helping mend a bruised reed. On behalf of Our Lord, he was receiving her gesture of love. Was it too much?

As I look out the window where I sit, I can see in the garden a most gorgeous array of flowers. Their colors are beyond my description. Last night as I looked into the western sky to behold the setting sun, I saw another display of colors beyond my description. Was this extravagant coloration too much? God does not think so!

The God who lavishes so much upon us delights to give. I do enjoy these words of the song-writer: "He giveth..and giveth... and giveth again." No, I become more convinced every day, that any measure of love we might return could never be too extravagant!

FATHER my heart responds. What a privilege to become extravagant! May I never be guilty, like so many of Your disciples, who question, "Why this waste?"

He Put His Arm Around Me

PROFESSOR STEWART BLACKIE. . . of Edinburgh University was lecturing one day when a student stood, holding the Bible in his left hand. The young man began reading a passage.

"Take your book in your **right** hand," the Professor scolded, "and be seated! You know my requirements in this class."

The student never answered a word, but merely held up his right arm. It had been severed at the wrist. The Professor hesitated a moment. His face bathed in tears, he went back to the student.

"I never knew about it," he said. Will you forgive me?"

Years later, when this story was told at a Bible conference, a man, with his right arm severed at the wrist, arose and came forward.

"I am the man that Professor Blackie led to Christ. But he never would have done it, if he had not first put his arms around me and made the wrong right!"

In the book of Acts the early believers were called the "people of the way." Those who observed were impressed by their different manner of life. It was what they saw, that caught everyone's attention. The act (of new birth) had become an attitude (truth) and produced a different way of living. Most likely it was this vitality and vibrancy in their living that caused the world around them to announce: here are the people who turn this world up-side-down. When Jesus announced "I am the way, the truth and the life," He never intended for us to be less than all three of these: The act (receiving life) becomes an attitude (truth) and then demonstrates a new way of living.

Professor Blackie took the low way and humbled himself. With him mercy was not a single act, it was also an attitude and a manner of life. When we seek to escape the embarrassment of the moment, we will perform an act of mercy. However, it seems evident that God had already brought the Professor to mercy as a way of living... and it was impressive.

God is ever pressing us to His larger window: Any act (of grace, mercy or peace) must become a daily attitude and produce a new way of living. Do I hear you sighing—'but that is so very difficult.'

That is why Jesus announced He was our source: "I am the Life, the Truth and the Way."

Only as Jesus lives His LIFE in us, and His TRUTH becomes our continual attitude—can He express His new WAY of living in us.

FATHER, my choice today is to BECOME MERCIFUL. I know that You are my sufficiency... always ready to supply my every need. Maybe at the close of this day... someone will announce: Today, I have seen another believer who has been demonstrating THE NEW AND LIVING WAY.

Greatness In Disguise

ON RETURNING FROM. . .
a general conference, Bishop Roberts applied to a Methodist family for a place to stay that night. He was, as usual, humble in dress dusty and weary. Upon arriving, the family assumed him to be a rustic traveler; they permitted him to put up and feed his horse and then take his seat in the living-room. Supper was over, and no one inquired if he had eaten on the way.

It so happened that the preacher of the circuit was stopping at the same house. He was young and frivolous, and spent the evening in gay conversation with the daughter of the family, alluding occasionally and contemptuously to the "old man" who sat silently in the corner.

The good Bishop, after sitting a long time, with no other attention than these allusions, retired to bed. The bedroom was over the sitting-room and, while praying with fatherly feeling for the careless young preacher, he still heard the jesting and rude laughter. At last, the family retired without devotions. The young preacher went up to sleep in the same room with the Bishop.

"Well, old man," he said as he got into bed, "Are you not asleep?"

"I am not, sir," replied the Bishop.

"Where have you come from?"

"From east of the mountains."

"From east of the mountains? What place?"

"Baltimore, "he responded.

"Baltimore—the seat of our general conference. Did you hear anything about it? We expect Bishop Roberts to stop here on his way home from the conference."

"Yes, sir," replied the Bishop humbly. "It ended before I left."

"Did you ever see Bishop Roberts?"

"Yes, sir, often. We left Baltimore together."

"You left Baltimore together? What's your name?"

"Roberts, sir."

"Roberts!... Excuse me, would you be related to the Bishop?"

'They usually call me Bishop Roberts, sir."

"Bishop Roberts! Bishop Roberts! Are you Bishop Roberts?"

The agitated young preacher was speechless and embarrassed. He implored the good man's pardon, insisted on calling up the family, and seemed willing to do anything to redeem himself.

The Bishop gave him an affectionate admonition, which he promised with tears never to forget. The venerable and compassionate Bishop knew the frivolity of youth. He gave the young preacher much fatherly advice and prayed with him, but would not allow the family to be called, though he had eaten nothing since breakfast.

The next morning, after praying again with the young man, he left before the family had risen. He wanted to spare them a mortifying explanation. At the next conference, the renewed, young itinerant called upon the Bishop. Weeping, he again acknowledged his error and became a useful minister. Bishop Roberts often alluded to the incident, but would never tell the name of the young preacher.

This story caught my attention, first, because I spent three years on the campus of Seattle Pacific University and lived in Roberts Hall, a dormitory named after this bishop; and secondly, because apart from the grace of God, in my younger years, I could have been that same careless preacher boy.

How faithfully God deals with us. A devoted man who had experienced much explained that God's dealings in his life reminded him of the two hands on the dial of the clock: The short hand of discipline and the long hand of mercy. Slowly and surely the hand of discipline must pass and speaks at each stroke. Yet over and over passes the long hand of mercy showering a twelve fold blessing for each stroke of discipline and trial. Both hands are fastened to one secure pivot: the great unchanging heart of Our Father who loves us too much to leave us the way we are.

FATHER, I do know by Your hand of discipline that unless I humble myself I will be humbled! But I also know from Your hand of mercy that whenever I make the right choices You will lift me up in ways I could not have expected. You are wholly TRUSTworthy.

"...ye younger, submit yourselves unto the elder. Yea, all of you be subject to one another. And be clothed with humility: for God resists the proud, and gives grace to the humble.

"Humble yourselves, therefore under the mighty hand of God, that he may exalt you in due time. (1 Peter 5:5-6)

Tears of Mercy

HENRY BOSCH EXPLAINS. . .

"If we don't feel sorrow in our heart over the fate of those who are spiritually lost, then we don't see the world as God sees it. Witnessing for Christ will be most effective when our words of testimony come from a heart of compassion.

One day David Garrick, a famous Shakespearean actor, was attracted to a gospel meeting. He was deeply moved to see tears freely coursing down the speaker's face. Suddenly an old woman raised a withered finger at the preacher and said, "Sir, I have heard you plead five times today on the various streets of this city, and five times I have seen your tears. Why do you weep?"

He replied that he couldn't help but cry with concern over the fearful condition of the lost. That tearful preacher known to the eastern colonies—was George Whitefield.

David Garrick later said, "As I listened to Whitefield, I saw his passion and his merciful heart. I knew he meant that without Christ people would die! When he came to the place where he could say nothing more, he reached up those mighty arms, and his voice seemed almost like a thunderstorm as he yearned over the people and said, "Oh! Oh!" Then Garrick concluded, "I would give my handful of gold sovereigns if I could say 'Oh' like that." (H.B.)

I believe I know what he meant! I can still recall hearing that kind of weeping when it flows from a merciful heart. One evening as we sat in our car at the railway station waiting for a friend to arrive, a man staggered along beside us who was obviously drunk —and showing all the marks of dissipation.

I imagined that he might be known as the town drunk, for others who observed his plight shouted out their disdain and disgust. I shall never forget my father-in-law who sat at my side. Suddenly "bowels of compassion" burst forth from his heart and he prayed, "Oh God, my Father! Here is some mother's son; here is somebody's brother. Maybe—he is some family's daddy whose children at home are crying, Where is our daddy tonight?'"

As you can see, I have never forgotten those groaning words that issued from his heart. He continued to pray: "My Father! Here is one of your fallen creation who has missed You and Your purpose for his life. All around us are folks who ridicule and scorn because they have never felt Your Father-heart of compassion. Father! Forgive them—forgive all of us—for our cold hearts and our coming so short of mercy as You are merciful."

Such weeping, such burden I have never forgotten. And I am now pondering if this is what the actor, David Garrick, felt when he explained "Oh, if I could sigh 'Oh!' like George Whitefield!"

Turn again our captivity, O Lord, as the streams in the south,
They that sow in tears shall reap in joy.
He that goes forth and weeps, bearing precious seed,
shall doubtless come again with rejoicing,
bringing his sheaves with him

There is much preaching and teaching today—and it is all good! And there is very much praying–even long prayers—yet there is this missing note: the broken heart that can weep tears and sigh 'oh' as Whitefield did.

FATHER, do I hear You saying to us: Someone needs to take his place. Will it be you?

Though sown in tears
Through weary years,
The seed will surely live;
Though great the cost,
It is not lost,
For God the fruit will give.

■ Anon.

The Whole Tree was White

THOUGH SEVENTY years have passed, there are a few illustrations my Dad used in his sermons which cling to my memory. Here is another of his favorites:

Three teenagers boarded a bus in New Jersey. Seated on the bus was a quiet, poorly dressed man who sat alone and silent. When the bus made its first stop, everybody got off except this one man, who remained aloof and alone. As the kids came back on the bus, one of them said something cheerful to him and he smiled shyly.

At the next bus stop, as everybody got off, the last teenager turned and said to the man, "Come on. Get off with us. At least stretch your legs."

So he got off. The teenagers invited him to have lunch with them. One of the young people said, "We are going to Florida for a weekend in the sun. It is nice in Florida, they say."

He said, "Yes, it is."

"Have you been there?"

"Oh, yes," he said, "I used to live there."

One said, "Weil, do you still have a home and family?"

He hesitated, "I—I don't know," he said, finally.

"What do you mean, you don't know?" the teenager persisted.

It was then that he felt free to share this painful story. Caught up by their warmth and sincerity, he shared:

"Many years ago, I was sentenced to Federal prison. I had a beautiful wife and wonderful children. When I left, I said to her, 'Honey, don't write to me. I won't write to you. The kids should not know that their dad is in prison. If you want to, go ahead and find another man—somebody who will be a good father to those boys.' Many, many years have now passed.

"I don't know if she kept her part of the bargain. I kept mine. Last week when I knew for sure I was getting out, I wrote a letter to our old address; it's just outside of Jacksonville. I said to her, 'If you are still living there and get this letter, if you haven't found anyone else, and if there is a chance of you taking me back—here is how you can let me know. I will be on the bus as it comes through town. I want you to take a piece of white cloth and hang it in the old oak tree right outside of town.' "

When they got back on the bus and they were about ten miles from Jacksonville, all the teenagers moved to this man's side of the bus and pressed their faces against the windows. Just as they came to the outskirts of Jacksonville there was the big oak tree. The teenagers let out a yell and they jumped out of their seats. They hugged each other and danced in the center of the aisle. All they said was, "Look at it! Look at it!" Not a single white cloth was tied to the tree. Instead, there was a white bedsheet, a white dress, a little boy's white trousers, and white pillowcases!

The whole tree was covered with dozens of pieces of white cloth! What could speak more loudly... that he was forgiven... forgiven! The entire family was out there with open arms, expressing mercy.

If our human family can demonstrate such mercy, consider how our Heavenly Father treats you and me, when He erases our past record.

FATHER, I join the great company of saints—who know by personal experience that You have been a merciful Father. Like two little puppy dogs that have been nipping at my heels, I can look back and say: surely goodness and mercy have followed me all the days of my life."

...according to His abundant mercy he hath begotten us again unto a lively hope..." (1 Peter 1:3)

She's My Friend

WHATEVER THEIR PLANNED TARGET. . . the mortar rounds landed in an orphanage run by a missionary group in a small Vietnamese village. The missionaries and one or two children were killed outright; several more children were wounded, including one young girl, about eight years old.

People from the village requested medical help from a neighboring town that had radio contact with the American forces. Finally, an American Navy doctor and nurse arrived in a jeep with only their medical kits. They established that the young girl was the most critically injured. Without quick action, she would die of shock and loss of blood.

A transfusion was imperative, and a donor with a matching blood type was required. A quick test showed that neither American had the correct type, but several of the uninjured orphans did.

The doctor spoke some pidgin Vietnamese, and the nurse a smattering of high-school French. Using that combination, together with much impromptu sign language, they tried to explain to their young, frightened audience that unless they could replace some of the girl's lost blood, she would certainly die. Then they asked if anyone would volunteer to give their blood to help.

Their request was met with wide-eyed silence. After several long moments, a small hand slowly and hesitantly went up, dropped back down, and then went up again.

"Oh, thank you," the nurse said in French. "What is your name?" "Heng," came the reply.

Heng was quickly laid on a pallet, his arm swabbed with alcohol, and a needle inserted in his vein. Through this ordeal Heng lay stiff and silent. After a moment, he let out a shuddering sob, quickly covering his face with his free hand.

"Is it hurting, Heng?" the doctor asked. Heng shook his head, but after a few moments another sob escaped, and once more he tried to cover up his crying. Again the doctor asked him if the needle hurt, and again Heng shook his head. But now his occasional sobs gave way to a steady, silent crying as he screwed his tightly-shut fist into his mouth to stifle his sobs.

The medical team was concerned. Something was obviously very wrong. At this point, a Vietnamese nurse arrived to help. Seeing the little one's distress, she spoke to him rapidly in Vietnamese, listened to his reply and answered him in a soothing voice. After a moment, Heng stopped crying and looked questioningly at the Vietnamese nurse.

When she nodded, a look of great relief spread over his face. Glancing up, the nurse said quietly to the Americans, "He thought he was dying. He misunderstood you. He thought you had asked him to give all his blood so the little girl could live."

"But why would he be willing to do that?" asked the Navy nurse. The Vietnamese nurse repeated the question to the little boy, who answered simply, "She's my friend."

We are not told whether little Heng had trusted Christ as His Savior. Perhaps he had! We do know that there remains in all mankind some of the original virtues of Adam before the fall. This virtue of mercy seems to be demonstrated in little Heng. The Apostle Paul explains this: *"Very rarely will anyone die for a righteous man, though for a good man someone might possibly dare to die."* Is that what we see in Heng?

What becomes even more wonderful—is the fact that our Lord Jesus was willing to die for us (not as friends, but) when we were enemies. That is **God's unspeakable mercy!** And He bids us who have been the objects of his mercy—to become His channels.

"Be merciful, as Your Father is merciful." (Lk 6:36)
"Blessed are the merciful, for they shall obtain mercy."

FATHER, it is my desire to be merciful, but it is not always in my strength. How can I show mercy when sometimes I feel like demanding justice? Then I hear Your words again: only as you know the abiding life—at the river of My grace—can you expect mercy to flow out through you to others. I will abide... that is my choice!

Three Kinds of Peace We Can Have

The Larger Window of Peace

Peace with God	Peace of God	Peace from God
Rom. 5:1	Phil. 4:7	2 Thess. 3:16
Eph. 2:14-17	Col. 3:15	1 Tim. 1:2

PEACE WITH GOD is available. God is looking for those who will receive His Son as their peace. Because of what Jesus did at the cross, God is now "preaching peace by Jesus Christ" (Acts 10:36). So the question is, Will men give up trying to make peace, and come as broken-hearted penitents and accept the peace God has already made; or, will they continue as enemies estranged from God?

PEACE OF GOD is available. A prominent judge observed: "It seems to me that people have more mental disorders today. Or is it just that I have more attention focused on such things? What would you advise as the best way to eliminate psychiatric problems?"

World-renowned Psychiatrist Dr. Crane answered him: "There would be much less strain on men and women if they teamed up with God as a daily partner. Indeed, in that event, psychiatry would almost pass out of existence. People who try to live independently and ignore God are soon overwhelmed with innumerable fears and worries. They become typical hypochondriacs, always fretting about gall bladders or ulcers or appendix or impending cancer. In teaming up with God, the human race would soon be able to throw off 50% of its ailments that counselors admit are psychological."

PEACE FROM GOD is what flows through us as we BECOME peace-makers. One day a pastor was counseling privately with a man. The closed door opened and a little boy entered the room. The pastor turned toward the boy and asked him a question: "Son, suppose your dad and mamma, would quarrel, what would you do? Would you, with your mamma fight against your dad; or would you help your dad against your mamma?" After a moment's silence, the son of the pastor gave this thoughtful answer: "I would stay in between and try to stop the fighting."

One Thing Thou Lackest

THE RICH YOUNG RULER. . . was the most difficult of all the cases with which the Master had to deal. If a man's character is obviously and glaringly deficient, it is easy to rebuke him. His conscience has prepared him for all that you can say. But if a man's character is attractive in so many respects that it puts your own to shame, it is extremely difficult to point out the flaws by which it is disfigured.

George Whitefield faced that difficulty. In traveling about the country and staying with all kinds of people, he made it his practice to deal kindly, yet faithfully, with all the members of the families when he was entertained.

In one town, however, he was the guest of a Colonel and his wife. His host, his hostess, and their daughters were so lavish in their hospitality, so considerate of his slightest needs, and so charming in all their conversation and behavior that Mr. Whitefield dreaded to say anything that might conceivably be construed as a rebuke.

The days went by! Although he felt that the gospel message with which he was entrusted had not pierced their conscience, yet not a word was said. The last night of the visit came, and the evangelist could not sleep.

"These people," he said to himself, "have been very kind to me, and I have not been faithful to them. I must do my duty before I go."

As he thought of it, however, he realized afresh the extreme difficulty and distrusted himself.

"When I see them face to face," he said, "my heart will fail me, and I shall leave without delivering my message."

He walked across to the window and an idea suddenly suggested itself. Across a frosty window pane glass he wrote, using his ring, the words—*"one thing thou lackest."*

And when he was about to leave, it was just as he feared. He could not bring himself to speak to such gracious people of the house as they showered their last kindness upon him. He left without expressing the one thought that was uppermost in his mind.

He had no sooner gone than the lady of the house, who greatly admired Whitefield, hurried to his room.

"I like," she said, "to look upon the place in which we have lodged so honored a guest."

Just then the inscription on the window pane caught her eye. It immediately and profoundly impressed her. She had heard that it was Mr. Whitefield's custom to deal personally with the members of the households with whom he stayed. She had thought it strange that he had never broached the gospel to them. Had they vexed him? Or, did he deem them unworthy of the precious gift that he offered with such earnestness to others? Such thoughts had greatly puzzled her. But now she thought she understood.

She called her daughters, "See!" she said, "See what Mr. Whitefield has written on the window. I thought that we must have offended him, but I see now that he was too tender in mind to speak to us. Call your Father!"

The Colonel joined them and read the words inscribed upon the glass, *"One thing thou lackest!"* He too, had been impressed by Mr. Whitefield's passionate entreaties in public and yet had marveled at his silence in the home. But now the light that had broken upon the mind of his wife illumined his also. And—so the record concludes—around the bed upon which the great preacher had tossed so restlessly, harassed by such great heart-searching and mental distress, they all knelt together. And there, within an hour of Mr. Whitefield's departure, they all sought and found peace with God—that one thing which, until then, they had lacked, yet of which Mr. Whitefield had found it so difficult to speak.

God has strange ways of answering our prayers. We need to realize that He has a greater concern for the lost than we do. I can believe when this news reached Whitefield there was a delightful inner peace that flooded his heart and he could say: "Thank You, my Father, for granting peace to their burdened hearts... and to mine!

No discipline seems pleasant at the time, but painful.
Later, however, it produces a harvest of righteousness
and peace for those who have been trained by it.

Copper Nails

WHAT IS A TROUBLED CONSCIENCE? By itself the conscience is simply a built-in monitor that alerts you when a thought or action may violate your personal moral "program," whatever that may be. The conscience does not force you into a choice, and it cannot tell you how to decide. Furthermore, it does not necessarily point you to the option that is in line with God's truth.

Only when you accept Christ as your Savior does the conscience function as God intends. Under the guidance of the Holy Spirit who lives in you the moment you trust in Jesus, the conscience becomes a powerful tool to help you make right choices within the context of Scripture. Instead of being instructed by a worldly system of values, your conscience is gradually reprogrammed according to God's value code.

Each Sunday the pastor had been preaching on the importance of a clear conscience, and urging upon his hearers the importance of confession of sin, and wherever possible, of making restitution for wrong done to others. At the close of the service, a young man, a member of the church, came up to him with a troubled countenance.

"Pastor," he explained, "you have put me in a sad fix. I have wronged another and I am ashamed to confess it or to try to put it right. You see, I am a boatbuilder, and the man I work for is an infidel. I have talked to him often about his need of Christ and have urged him to come to hear you preach, but he scoffs and ridicules it all. Now, I have been guilty of something that, if I should acknowledge it to him, will ruin my testimony forever."

He then explained that sometime ago he started to build a boat for himself in his own yard. In this work copper nails are used because they do not rust in the water. These nails are quite expensive; and he had been carrying home quantities of them to use on his boat. He knew it was stealing, but he tried to salve his conscience by telling himself that the owner had so many he would never miss them, and beside he was not being paid all that he thought he deserved. Now, this sermon had brought him to face the fact that he was just a common thief, for whose dishonest actions there was no excuse.

"But," he continued, "I cannot go to my boss and tell him what I have done or offer to pay for those nails I have used and return the rest. If I do he will think I am just a hypocrite. And yet those copper nails are digging into my conscience. I know I shall never have peace until I put this matter right."

For weeks the struggle went on. Then one night he exclaimed, "Pastor, I've settled for the copper nails and my conscience is relieved at last."

"What happened when you confessed to your employer what you had done?" asked the pastor.

"Oh, he looked queerly at me, then exclaimed, 'George, I always did think you were just a hypocrite, but now I begin to feel there might be something in this Christianity after all. Any religion that would make a dishonest workman come back and confess that he had been stealing copper nails and offer to settle for them, must be worth having.'"

After asking permission, the pastor felt led to share this story many times and almost invariably people came to explain how 'copper nails' in one form or another had been digging them.

One lady confessed, "I have had copper nails on my conscience too."

"Why, surely you are not a boatbuilder!"

"No, but I am a book-lover, and I have kept a number of books which belong to a friend who earns far more than I do. I decided last night I must get rid of those 'copper nails.' So I took all the books back to her and confessed my sin."

On one occasion pastor told this at a High School chapel service. The next day the principal saw him and said, "As a result of that 'copper nails' story, ever so many stolen fountain pens, and other things have been returned to their rightful owners."

We must be clear. Reformation and making restitution have no saving merit. But it is evident throughout Scripture that peace was missing in those hearts who have avoided making things right with others. In many of his Psalms David explains how a gnawing conscience troubled him through the night hours.

Would you consider memorizing these valuable verses and then meditating on them:

"Blessed is he whose transgressions are forgiven whose sins are covered.

Blessed is the man whose sin the Lord does not count against him and in whose spirit is no deceit.

When I kept silent, my bones wasted away through my groaning all day long.
For day and night Your hand was heavy upon me; my strength was sapped as in the heat of summer.

Then I acknowledged my sin to You and did not cover my iniquity. I said, 'I will confess my transgression to the Lord'—and You forgave the guilt of my sin.

Therefore, let everyone who is godly pray to You while You may be found."
(Ps. 32:1-6, NIV).

Father, I choose to be completely honest before You. Nothing can be hidden from Your eye. I acknowledge _____ has been troubling me. I thank You for hearing me, and for cleansing me from this. It has gnawed on my conscience too long. I will expect the peace that comes from a heart that is clear before You. I know this is the right thing to do. I appreciate Your patience with me.

The Judge Was Arrested

ABOUT THE TIME WE MORTALS THINK. . .
we have God's ways figured out, He doesn't conform to our formula, and works according to a higher law which we do not understand. Surely the Apostle Paul was sounding this note when he wrote: *"How unsearchable are his judgments, and his ways past finding out! For who hath known the mind of the Lord? or who hath been His counselor?"*

In this story we shall take a peek at that "higher law." How does it work? In 17th century England Pastor Richard Baxter was much beloved during his 50 years as pastor. He explained that he preached with great intensity because he saw himself as a dying man ministering to dying people. He always spoke as if he were preaching his last sermon and as if his listeners were hearing their last message.

And what a full schedule he maintained! Each Monday and Tuesday he spent 7 hours instructing the children of his parish, not omitting even one child. On Wednesday, he went from house to house to make sure that the material needs of the widows, the aged, and the infirm were met. During the rest of the week he prepared his sermons and wrote a total of 150 books.

As a result of the Holy Spirit working through his ministry, the town of Kidderminster was transformed. It had been a place of sexual immorality and vice, but it became a village in which nearly every household honored God, read the Bible, and prayed. The generations that now look back on Baxter's consuming zeal understand why he reaped such rich spiritual harvest.

Consider this one example of his effective ministry. One evening as Baxter was riding to a village some distance from his home to preach, night came on quickly and he missed his way. Finally, he saw a lighted house near the roadside. He went to the door and asked to stay overnight. The master of the house consented. During the evening meal, the gentleman asked his guest what his business was.

Baxter quietly replied, "I am a man-catcher, sir."

"Oh," said the man, "you are the very one I want. I am the Justice of the Peace, and I want to catch Richard Baxter who will preach tomorrow morning in a house nearby."

Baxter did not reveal his identity. He agreed to go with his host to the meeting. Early the next day, they went to the house where the people had gathered to hear Dick Baxter preach. The Justice of peace thought that Dick Baxter had not yet appeared.

After waiting some time he said, "I suppose Baxter has heard of my plans to arrest him, and is not going to fulfill his engagement."

Everyone waited quietly for a while. Eventually the Justice suggested that perhaps his guest should offer a prayer and talk to the people. Then Mr. Baxter opened the meeting! He began with a stirring prayer. Then He delivered a heart-searching sermon. The Justice was melted to tears. It was soon evident that God had come to their meeting that day! At the close of his message, Richard Baxter turned to the Justice and said:

"I am the Dick Baxter you are looking for! Take me!"

But the Justice could not arrest Dick Baxter. He himself had been arrested as the power of God's Word had broken his hard heart. Instead of persecuting Baxter, the Justice trusted Christ right on the spot and became a supporter of Baxter.

It is one of God's mysterious ways—that He so often comes as a friend of sinners to those who do not want Him to invade their lives. In this instance, He came incommunicado—Richard Baxter became a friend to this Judge—and thus opened his eyes. It is exactly the same with our Lord Jesus—who first becomes a friend of sinners, so they will allow Him to enlighten their hearts.

The master strategy of the Enemy has always been to present an ugly caricature of God. Those who accept this deception are wholly convinced they have a right to reject His claims on their life. However, the opposite is true:

To really know Him is to love Him.
To really love Him is to obey Him.
To really obey Him is to worship His ways.

FATHER, I will accept this exhortation from Job:
"Acquaint now thyself with Him, and be at peace: thereby good shall come unto thee." (Job 22:21)

The Prodigal Returns

ROBERT ROBINSON, A POOR ORPHAN wandered from place to place, never calling anywhere home. Then one night, the Holy Spirit led him into a tent meeting. The well- known evangelist, George Whitefield, was speaking on the subject of Jesus' love for poor, lost sinners.

Robert's heart was touched. He was baptized, enrolled in a ministerial college, and graduated as a Methodist minister. In 1758 at the age of 23, Robert wrote the words to the hymn: "Come, Thou Fount of Every Blessing," first published as a poem.

Years passed, and Robert lost his fellowship with the Lord. He gradually drifted away from his calling as a minister. One day he found himself traveling in a stagecoach with a Christian woman who insisted on talking with him about God. He was feeling especially low, so he tried to avoid speaking to her, but she persisted in speaking to him.

"You should hear the words to this incredible poem I found." Then she read his poem to him, not realizing that he was the man who had written it years earlier. When the woman had finished reading, Robert tried to change the subject. Still the woman raved on about the poem and its beautiful message.

Finally, in exasperation, Robert blurted out, "Madam, I know the words to the poem quite well. I am the poor, unhappy man who composed that hymn many years ago, and I would give a thousand worlds if I could enjoy those same feelings I felt then."

Stunned by Robert's confession, the embarrassed woman dared not speak again for the rest of the trip. By the time the stagecoach arrived at its destination, the Holy Spirit had been working in Robert's heart. He confessed his sin, received cleansing, returned to the ministry and served his Lord from that day until his death in 1790.

FATHER, it is heartening to know when one is out of tune with You as Robert was, that You are eagerly waiting for wandering sons to return. Perhaps someone reading this, needs to do that now!

"...be diligent that ye may be found of Him in peace, without spot and blameless..."

There was Peace in Her Valley!

IT WAS A HOT. . . humid morning. There was no sound in the operating room of a New York hospital except the droning of an electric fan. An emergency had played havoc with the surgeon's schedule.

The atmosphere in the room reflected his tension and irritability. The nurse spoke assuringly to the young woman on the operating table, "Breathe naturally, and count slowly." She wondered if the lovely girl, so relaxed and smiling, knew what a serious operation she was facing.

"I would rather say the Twenty-third Psalm, if you don't mind," the patient said quietly.

The doctor's face reflected surprise and sudden interest. "Yes, say it," he told the patient, "I also need to hear the Twenty-third Psalm this morning."

The quiet of the operating room was broken only by the confident voice of the young woman:. *"The Lord is my shepherd: I shall not want,"* began the young woman slowly and clearly.

Suddenly, peace and serenity had filled that operating room. Everyone seem to be tuned in to hear each word. In that simple setting, nurses and doctors listened to the beauty of that glorious old psalm as if they had never heard it before.

"Yea, though I walk through the valley of the shadow of death, I will fear no evil, for thou art with me; thy rod and thy staff, they comfort me."

Her voice was growing softer... she spoke... more slowly.

"Hold it!" the surgeon requested. "I want to hear all of it!"

The voice trailed off... and then...all was still.

Misty-eyed, but apparently refreshed in spirit, the surgeon nodded, and the operating room sprang into action as the patient slipped into the etherized unknown—peaceful and comforted.

FATHER, I can realize why she was fully prepared. She was walking into the valley. But she was not alone! She was drawing from her reservoir of God's Word. Help me to develop a reservoir for such a time!

The Before and the After

HENRY SUSO WAS KNOWN. . . throughout his part of Germany for deep spirituality. That is, until one day when he heard a knock on the door. A strange woman stood there with a babe in her arms which she thrust into his arms saying, "Here, you have the fruit of your sin."

Suso had never before seen the woman. He was as innocent as a dove. The woman hastened away leaving him with the tiny babe. The news of what had happened went through the town like a flash. There was nothing... nothing he could do!

"So this is the man we had revered so holy! What a hypocrite! what a fraud!"—was the noisy echo about the town.

Suso was crushed. He groaned like a dying man. What was he to do. He withdrew to a desert place and called upon the Lord, telling Him it was more than he could bear.

"What shall I do, Lord?" he cried in his pain and shame. "You know that I am innocent."

The answer came to him with perfect clearness and finality— "What shall you do? Do as I did. Suffer because of the sins of others and say nothing."

Suso saw the cross. With acceptance, peace came to his troubled soul. He returned to his home, took the child, sweetly and humbly cared for the little one, and lovingly reared her as if she were his own daughter, never saying a word in self-defense.

Years later the unknown woman returned to publish abroad Suso's innocence, but God's work was done. Suso had been conformed to the image of God's Son. God's victory in him was achieved. All that Suso had been before was but a dim shadow of the qualities developed in him **after** accepting God's way of the cross.

Great peace have they that love thy law and nothing... nothing shall offend them. Charles Spurgeon shares his secret for such:

"I looked at Jesus, and the Dove of Peace flew into my heart.
I looked at the Dove and Peace flew away."

FATHER, I know there are no shortcuts for Your dealing with my inner life. I choose to accept the breaking that will deliver me from being pre-occupied with myself and my little world.

Holding on to the Spikes

SEVERAL MONTHS HAD PASSED. . . and I greeted a friend who had recently trusted Christ as His Savior. As my arm reached out to him, I asked, "How are you doing?"

"Well," he explained, "I'm having quite a struggle. You know it isn't easy! But I'm doing the best I can to keep myself saved!"

Immediately, as I heard these words, I knew he needed some help. So we sat down and I explained that many years ago I had had the same problem. I was trying to keep myself saved... until I understood what God did for Noah. I explained this difference: Noah was not **trying**, but **trusting;** Noah was not **hanging on** to the ark, but **resting in** the ark. I continued to explain what I had discovered:

Noah is a good example of one whom God declared righteous simply because of his faith. It was Noah's trusting what God had said, that led Noah to prepare an ark for the saving of his household—even when there appeared to be no evidence of rain or a coming flood.

After the ark was finished, *"The Lord said unto Noah, Come thou and all thy house **into the ark**, for thee have I seen righteous in this generation"* (Gen. 7:1).

Inside the ark, everyone was secure until the deluge was over. Remember, Noah and his household were shut in by God, for God Himself had closed the door. The same hand that shut them in also shut all out, including the whole unbelieving antediluvian world. The ark—a type of Christ—itself bore the brunt of the storm, while everyone inside rested safe and secure.

Then I asked my friend, "Suppose when the ark was completed God had said, *"Now Noah, get eight large spikes and drive them into the side of the ark."*

"Imagine," I continued, "that Noah drove those spikes into the side of the ark as he was commanded. What if Noah had then announced to his family members, 'Come, each one of you in my house, take hold of these spikes, and if you can hang on desperately until the end of the flood, you will be saved!' "

A smile appeared on the face of my friend.

"How long, I asked him, "do you think Noah and his family would have been able to hang on? Can you imagine each one desperately grasping his own spike, holding on for dear life! How long! The waters poured down from heaven! Finally the ark was lifted up! Think of the terrific strain on the joints and muscles as the ark made its perilous voyage through the raging waters.

After several minutes, I think I can hear Noah calling to his wife, 'My dear, how is it going? I trust you have enough strength to hang in there!'

"And Noah's wife calls back, 'I'm holding on. Do pray for me that I might be able to hold out and endure to the end!'

"Soon I can hear poor Mrs. Ham crying out, 'It's no use! I can't hang on any longer. I am going to lose my hold,' she screams. Finally she loses her grip and is swept away by the flood."

As I looked straight into my friend's eyes, I asked him, "How long do you suppose it would take before each of them would be swept away by the swirling flood waters?"

I explained how I had for many years assumed that it was God who saved me, **yet** I thought it depended on me to "keep myself saved,"—if I faithfully hung onto Him. One day, I realized God had called me into the ark; that is—He had placed me in Christ. In Christ as my Ark, I was resting safely and securely, being absolutely separated from the waters of judgment.

Truth has a wonderful, liberating effect. The moment my friend saw it he recognized that the finished work of Christ was complete for him; he took my hand and firmly announced:

"From now on, I'm resting **in Christ as my Ark**! I'll never again tell anyone that I'm trying to keep myself saved."

"Thou wilt keep him in perfect peace,
whose mind is stayed on thee;
because he trusteth in thee."

Yes, my Father—that gives me great confidence that You will protect me during the storms of life. Help me not to hang onto anything—feelings or possessions or friends—as my security. I'll not even need not to seek peace, for I have Jesus, who is my peace. He is enough!

Why Uncle Gave Up The Ministry

THE FOLLOWING SAD. . .
but true story concerns a wonderful jolly, beloved man, who was over six feet four and probably weighed close to three hundred pounds. He was also very well educated (Colgate University, Doctor of Divinity) and in the early 1900s became a full-time Baptist minister. A kindly, gentle man despite his size, Uncle Alden Bentley's only real fault seemed to be that he was terribly clumsy.

As a young minister, he was paying a pastoral call one day on a woman in Dillon, South Carolina, when he inadvertently sat on her Chihuahua, Twinkie, and killed it. As the lady searched and called for her dog throughout the house, Uncle Alden felt underneath his hip. Tragically he realized what he had done; he panicked and slipped the dead dog into his coat pocket. Although he was devastated, he could not bring himself to tell the woman what had happened.

Five years later, he returned to the same home for an overnight visit and resolved to unburden himself by finally telling the woman exactly what had happened to Twinkie. She had just had her guest room re-papered and had hung brand-new curtains. To make Uncle feel welcome, she had placed on the bedside table a large pitcher of ice water and a glass, as well as a pen and bottle of ink, so he could work on his sermon before retiring.

Uncle liked to sleep with the window open, so he got up in the night to open it. As he did, he knocked over what he assumed to be a full glass of water. Then, groping along the walls in an unsuccessful search for the light switch, he retraced his steps several times before raising the window and settling back on the bed for the night.

When he opened his eyes the next morning, he was horrified. The fresh wallpaper on two walls was covered with great black blobs. The crisp white curtains were thoroughly smudged with the prints of Uncle's huge paws. It had not been the water-glass he'd overturned during the night—it had been the ink bottle!

In a shaken state of mind and knowing he must face his hostess, Uncle dressed hurriedly and started down the stairs outside the guest room. As he approached the landing, his foot slipped.

Reaching wildly for support he grabbed the nearest object, which happened to be a beautiful electric brass candelabra mounted on the stairwell wall. The fixture was hissing and smoking as he ripped it from the wall and toppled down to the landing below, still clutching it in his hand.

"Are you hurt?" His hostess cried as she rushed to Uncle's side. "No," declared Uncle as he rose to do his feet, "but I have demolished your home."

With that, he quickly walked out the front door. At the end of the walk, he turned and blurted to his hostess with deep reverence, "Twinkie had a Christian burial."

Uncle then retired from the ministry and became a teacher of philosophy for many years at a private preparatory school in Massachusetts. It is important to note that Uncle left the pulpit but not his faith in Christ. We are told that he faithfully attended church and was known by all as a delightful Christian, though for years he carried the haunting memory of that episode.

At this moment it is not our concern whether uncle found his niche as a professor. That may have been God's best for him, and then it may have been a second best. What I wish to capture from this story is the consequences that come from our failure to quickly respond to the monitions of the Spirit working in our heart. Uncle knew what he should do, but he waited and waited.

I rather think this might be the sad plight of many who have a "Twinkie-episode" hidden in their past history. For many years they have wondered about the Lord's dealings in their life. At that first moment, Uncle should have followed through and openly acknowledged what happened to Twinkie. Thus he would have avoided years of soul-anguish—simply by heeding God's voice to confess it immediately—and cleared his conscience.

When I trust Christ, it is important to consider what God does in my spirit, and then understand what He continues doing in my soul, (mind, emotions, will).

* Once my spirit is saved on the basis of faith, my salvation is settled, but my soul is being saved (renewed) as I am following Him and daily obeying His Word (1 Pet. 1:22; James 1:21-22).

* My spirit is saved (quickened) because Christ lays down His life for me, and He immediately comes to indwell my spirit, but my soul is being saved (transformed) as I deny myself (Lk. 9:23).

* Receiving salvation of spirit is the beginning of my faith; receiving salvation of my soul is the end of my faith (1Pet. 1:9).

It will bring a new carefulness of attitude and purpose when we realize how important it is to accept the Lord's dealings with us immediately. Hearing and obeying His voice is not optional if we really desire the peace of God, and if we want to be ready to participate with Him when He establishes His future kingdom.

Whoever lives wholly to indulge his soul pleasures in this age will have gained what this world offers; but it seems certain he will lose much, very much privilege in the age to come. (See Matt. 16:25-26) The Apostle Paul exhorts us: "...if we suffer, we shall also reign with Him..."

FATHER, I do not want to develop a "suffering complex," or assume that You are against enjoyment in this present life. Yet the more I walk with You in close fellowship, the more I realize any true enjoyment comes not from seeking it, but rather in seeking Your face and knowing You more intimately; therein is the deepest enjoyment that truly satisfies.

It is no small thing that You have enrolled us in life's schoolroom, that we might "learn obedience" even as our Lord Jesus learned by the things he suffered. As Uncle Alden discovered from his "Twinkie-episode," let me learn not to put off what I need to handle today. Surely the alternative to obedience is not freedom, but the tyranny of a troubled conscience. Do I hear you reminding me to face some issue—right now?

Tools or Toys...

BY JAMIE BUCKINGHAM

I'm having a hard time enjoying my Flilpino house-guest. Already his presence has upset my way of living—a way in which I have grown very comfortable. The alternatives are not pleasant; either get rid of him or change my way of living.

I first met Aley Gonzalez three years before my first visit to the southernmost island of the Archipelago, Mindanao. An ex-boxer with more than a hundred professional fights under his bantam-weight-belt, this middle aged, tough-as-coconut-husk, brown-skinned Filipino was preaching like he fought in the ring—both hands jabbing, feet dancing and always boring in for the knock-out punch. With the aid of a vintage motorcycle and motorized outrigger canoe, he would go into some of the most inaccessible places in the island chain, starting churches and training pastors.

His average salary was fifty pesos a month (about seven dollars) and his entire wardrobe consisted of three pair of pants, some shirts, a cheap nylon jacket and a pair of rubber slaps.

Few Americans ever visit his out-of-the-way location in the province of Agusan del Norte. To get there you go seven hundred miles south from Manila, cross two volcanos, through the straits at Mactan, take a jeep ride through the rain forests to the coastal barrio of Cabadbaran. Those of us who had visited there had encouraged Aley to visit the States. It would surely broaden his perspective and make him a better preacher. Or, so we thought.

Then Aley arrived at my Florida home. My son Tim had worked that summer and saved money for an expensive new slalom water ski. Knowing how much Aley loved the water (we had spent some happy hours swimming together in the China Sea) I took him with us for a late afternoon ride on our new boat.

On the way to the marina we passed a golf course.

"Why do those men hit that little ball with those sticks?" he asked. "Does somebody hire them to do that?"

I started to give him an explanation but realized it sounded foolish, so I stopped. "We have a lot of people in America who do odd things," I mumbled.

Aley nodded. He understood.

"In the Philippines we hear there are many Americans without work. When jobs become more plentiful they will probably stop this foolishness." I didn't have the heart to tell him that only the rich could afford to be fools.

Aley was impressed with my boat.

"It is very expensive," he said softly, running his hands along the sleek fiberglass deck. "It must have cost twenty thousand pesos. But what do you use it for? Do your sons and daughters fish for a living?"

He could tell I was having trouble with the answer.

"Perhaps you and your wife go up and down the river and preach the gospel to all those out-of-work people swinging their sticks at the balls?" he asked, knowing that somewhere I had hidden a sensible answer.

When I explained we used the boat only to pull water skiers and for some sport fishing, he was startled. I could tell he was thinking of the thirty-two miles he had to paddle his outrigger just to get to the small village of San Jose where he preached the Gospel. And here I was with this sleek red and white fiberglass beauty. He turned his eyes away and said nothing.

Coming back, we stopped at the home of a friend who has three motorcycles in the garage. Aley's eyes danced with excitement, thinking of his battered old Kawasaki.

"These people must go many places helping the poor, feeding the hungry and preaching the Gospel," he said approvingly.

When I explained that although these people belonged to the church they weren't active Christians, he was startled. "You have church members who do not preach? How can this be? The Bible says all church members should be preaching the Gospel. What then do they use these motorcycles for?"

I explained they were dirt bikes, used only to roar around the woods, going no place. I saw that same pensive look move across his face like clouds over the sun. "There are many things about America which I need to learn," he said, amazed.

I drove home a different way. I didn't want him to see the yachts on the river, the dune buggies in the driveways, or the imposing church buildings which sit idle except for a few feeble groans on Sunday morning. I didn't want to face any more of his questions. It was the same feeling I had many years ago when as a young idealist, I attended a church service when they dedicated a seventy-five-thousand-dollar stained-glass window—to the glory of God. But I have mellowed since then.

Aley was too kind to say anything to me. But last night I couldn't help but see the expression on his face when he looked in my closet and saw all those shoes. I haven't been sleeping well recently. (J.B.)

This struggle Jamie describes is most common. We allow the closet of our life to be cluttered with things; yet many of us honestly want the heart-discipline to choose tools instead of toys. Perhaps I need to explain that tools are things that one uses to fulfill his service for God. Tools are very necessary and are the blessing of the Lord. Toys are things I acquire to satisfy my own pleasures or whims; toys are self serving things, not actually wrong—just like frosting on the cake which can be a problem for my health. So, it really boils down to this: everything I possess is either a tool or a toy.

Usually I have to convince myself—and God—that I really do know the difference! Yes, I really do want to choose tools that fulfill His purpose and I want to avoid toys that merely indulge me.

We are back to square one again: my need to daily hear God's voice and then obey. Only as I live in daily fellowship with God can I discern tools from toys. It is not a mental gymnastic, but rather a peace of heart that comes when I seek His face and desire only to please my Father.

I must be quick to explain: my Father is not a kill-joy who deliberately withholds things that are enjoyable. Often I have heard my Father whisper, "you're harder on yourself than I am. You may buy that, if it can be a tool to make you more effective: but you must be very careful to trust me that it will remain a tool."

FATHER, the closer I get to Your heart, I realize that You delight to share "exceedingly above that which I can ask or think" You do not withhold things that are enjoyable, except that You know when my life is cluttered and—I am distracted from enjoying You. To really know You is to love Your ways and your Word. I accept Paul's exhortation to Timothy:
"Charge them that are rich in this world, that they be not highminded, nor trust in uncertain riches, but in the Living God, who giveth us richly all things to enjoy."

Passing The Examination

THREE O'CLOCK ONE morning a missionary candidate climbed the steps to the examiner's home. He was shown into the study where he waited until eight o'clock for an interview. Upon arriving, the old clergyman proceeded to ask some questions:

"Can you spell?"

"Yes, Sir," was the reply.

"All right, spell baker."

"Baker, b-a-k-e-r."

"Fine. Now do you know anything about figures?" he asked.

"Yes, Sir, something."

"How much is twice two?"

"Four," replied the lad.

"That's splendid," returned the old man. "I believe you have passed. I will see the board tomorrow."

At the board meeting he explained this account of the interview. "He has all the qualifications of a missionary:

"First, I tested him on his self-denial. I told him to be at my house at three o'clock in the morning. He left a warm bed and came out in the cold without a word of complaint.

"Second, I tried him on promptness. He appeared on time.

"Third, I examined him on patience. I made him wait five hours to see me after telling him to come at three."

"Fourth, I tested him on temper. He was very peaceful, even though I treated him very poorly. He failed to show any ill temper and did not question the delay.

"Fifth, I tried his humility. I asked him questions that a five-year- old could answer, and he showed no indignation. So you can recognize he has some character qualities that will make him a committed servant."

It is now more than fifty years ago that my late wife left for India as a single missionary. When leaving, her missionary executive smiled: "I know you have your OUTFIT all ready, but I'll be praying about more your INFIT. When I married her seven years later, I discovered she did have—the most wonderful Indwelling Christ.

Did He Do it Right ?

THE EVENING SERVICE. . .
had ended. Most of the congregation had left, but a few remained to visit. Then one young lady approached me, quite pensive... and it seemed... hesitant. I could tell that she was troubled. I assumed the Holy Spirit might be speaking to her. I asked her softly, "Is there something I can help you with?"

She did not respond immediately, but very slowly she said, "I am not sure! Many times when I sit in a meeting like this, I'm full of questions! I have no assurance! I am not sure about my salvation. I'm not sure I did it right."

I urged her to explain what she meant.

"It has been many years ago that I responded to an invitation. I went forward to give my heart to the Lord. I've graduated from Bible School. teach Sunday School each week. I know I love the Lord and want to serve Him. But I'm still not sure about my personal salvation.

"I have looked back," she continued, "to that time years ago when I was a teenager, when I accepted Christ into my life. I had resisted God's calling. I did not want to become part of that 'peculiar group who said they were saved.' I really wanted to continue my 'good times and do my own thing.' Then, when God seemed to move into our teen-age group, many were saved, and it seemed evident that many lives were changed. I was one of the last to respond to become a Christian. For many months I moved along with our teen-age group. We were so excited because we all seemed to enjoy a relationship with the Lord Jesus, and with one another. In due time, I felt that God was calling me into His service.

"Now, after several years have passed and I've moved away from that group, many questions keep coming—many doubts arise! I'm really not sure I am saved; I lack peace that others have.

"I have so often questioned! When I responded to that invitation, did I really mean it? Or did I just follow my friends? Was I really sincere? Did I really confess all my sins? Maybe I held out on some thing God really wanted? Did I really make Jesus Lord of my life? Did I really open the door of my heart fully, so Jesus could come in. Maybe... maybe I didn't do something right?

"Perhaps I was moved by emotion and the pressure to be part of my group, and I should have weighed it more seriously whether I was really willing to pay the price."

Tears were flowing! It was evident this had been an ongoing struggle for some time. I suggested that we sit down and talk:

"You will forgive my seemingly bold confidence," I said to her, "but I am sure I can help you settle some very basic issues." She looked at me so hopefully.

"I believe your testimony," I explained, "that you trusted Christ and His shed blood for forgiveness. Surely you are a new creature in Christ, and the Lord Jesus did come into your heart, and it seems evident that the indwelling Spirit has been working in your life."

It was not the plainness of her life, nor the meekness of her spirit, but her manifest choice to please Him—all this together convinced me that she had experienced regeneration. But she was not clear in her assurance of salvation, because she did not understand the difference between regeneration and justification before God.

I quickly drew a little visual sketch and explained the difference between

WHAT GOD HAS DONE **IN** US and

WHAT GOD HAS DONE **FOR** US.

Her eyes were wide open with hope, as I explained, "You do belong to Him. But you are perhaps like thousands who have become confused. It is my deep regret that many well meaning servants of the Lord place more emphasis on what we must do rather than on what Christ has already done for them. For example they emphasize that you must—

" 'Accept Jesus as your Savior...,' or 'give your heart to the Lord...,' or 'confess all your sins so He will forgive...,' or 'be sure to make Him Lord of your life...,' or 'be ready to turn away from your sinful past...'

"Now, actually there is nothing wrong with all these exhortations—only that your attention is fixed upon what you must do in order to be saved. All these years your attention has been fixed on your part, and God wants you to recognize what has already been done for you on the cross, nineteen hundred years ago when Christ died as your substitute to pay your sin debt.

"Let me ask you this simple question: When God looked down on Calvary and saw what His Son had finished in His death...

...Was God completely satisfied? Yes, of course!

...Did Jesus do it perfectly right? Surely it was right!

...Did God accept the perfect blood that Jesus shed? Of course!

"Now, when your faith rests on what Jesus has done for you—His finished work—God simply says: 'you are justified, declared righteous.' You must never confuse what the Lord Jesus has done for you on the cross, with what He has done in you! As you keep your eyes turned out toward Him, the Holy Spirit will work within you."

It was a wonderful moment when I heard her shout out: "I see it! I see it! God is satisfied! And if He is satisfied, then I should be satisfied with Jesus and His finished work. Oh—I'll no longer be questioning whether I did anything right or wrong. It's what He did that really counts. He did everything right."

I went on to explain that we could never confess all our sins we committed before we trusted Him. There are too many to remember. She could agree to that. So the only confession we can make is, God be merciful to me a sinner! God will accept that confession.

However, after we are saved, and belong to Him, we are exhorted to confess any sins in order to maintain our fellowship with Him. Once you have a relationship with the Father, you should "walk in the light" to enjoy continuing fellowship. (1 Jn. 1:7)

She left that evening with an assurance that only God can give. She had come to "see and to fully trust the finished work of Christ." For many years she had peace with God. Now she enjoyed the peace of God and this gave her a new confidence in speaking to others.

The Holy Spirit is faithful to convict the seeker of his sin. We must be discerning and quick to turn their attention to thank the One who has fully paid the sin-debt they could never pay.

So, it is important to recognize this distinction between regeneration and justification. One is subjective and places the emphasis on what man must do. The other is objective and places the emphasis on what Christ has already done. In the next story we will consider what God does in us: what is His regenerating work.

FATHER, help me to use wisdom in turning seeking hearts outward to see and trust what Christ has already done for them—and give thanks!

APPENDIX B

The Apostle Paul is very clear in writing to the church at Corinth:

"And such were some of you; but ye are washed, but ye are sanctified, but ye are justified in the name of the Lord Jesus, and by the Spirit of our God." In this window we explain the difference between...

What God does **FOR US** Justification	What God does **WITH US** Sanctification	What God does **IN US** Regeneration

1...the regenerating work of the Holy Spirit is God's work IN US when we receive Christ as our personal savior. *"As many as received Him, to them He gave the right to become children of God..."* Paul explains: "...He saved us, through the washing of regeneration and the renewing of the Holy Spirit." Just as it is difficult to explain the wind, so it is with the Holy Spirit's coming into us at our new birth.

2...the sanctifying work of the Holy Spirit is to set apart whatever has touched the altar (the cross). Once we were "in Adam" but now because we were crucified, buried and resurrected with Christ on the cross, He sees us "in Christ". Thus, we are set apart from our old world and unto God for His purposes. What God does WITH US—in separating us unto Himself—is first a crisis-position in which we stand (1 Cor.1;2) and becomes a process as we walk in sanctification and honor (1 Thess.4:4).

3...the justifying work of God is to reckon righteousness to our account, when in simple faith we look away from ourselves to see what Christ has accomplished FOR US in His finished work on the Cross. God was fully satisfied with His work; it is not our enthroning Christ in our hearts but that He enthroned the Lord Jesus at His right hand in Heaven. So in justification, we become totally occupied with Him, and with what Christ did FOR US 1900 years ago on the Cross. Now our faith has an Object outside ourselves and outside our experience!

Please Explain To Me...

NO ONE DOUBTED THAT. . .
the atheist was a brilliant speaker. In debate, he could generally make his opponent, however brilliant, trip himself up and look utterly ridiculous. As a lecturer, his arguments were subtly convincing, and his ability to mislead hearers was proven by the spread of infidelity wherever he gave his infamous addresses.

One evening he was giving a lecture in a large mining town. He noticed in his audience one man who listened most intently. This man was still wearing his grimy miner's work clothes, and his massive frame and muscles showed him to be a man of unusual physical strength.

The lecturer argued against the divine inspiration of the Bible, against Jesus Christ as God's Son, and against Christianity as the logical consequence of such beliefs. Looking at his audience and feeling confident that he had destroyed any faith his hearers had in such theories—as he labeled them—he ended his address.

"Now," he said, "I'm sure that I have succeeded in explaining to you the myth that is called the religion of Jesus Christ."

He had hardly finished when the miner, whom he had previously noted, rose slowly to his feet. Though dressed in grimy clothes, he demanded respect as he towered over his neighbors. His voice boomed through the hall as he addressed the infidel speaker.

"Sir," he said, "I'm only a working man and I don't know your fancy word 'myth.' But these people know me! They know that until three years ago I was the toughest man in town. They know that up till that time I had a miserable home. I neglected my wife and children. I cursed, I swore. I drank all my wages, and whoever opposed me soon felt the force of my fist.

"Then someone came along and told me of the mercy of God to poor sinners. He gave me a glimpse of Christ Jesus dying on Calvary's cross for lost wretches like me. He lifted me up with hope and faith in the very things that you now call myths. I believed those very things that you now deny, and through my new-found trust in the cleansing power of the Savior's blood, my life was changed. These folks can tell you that my life is now completely different. We have a happy home. I love my wife and children. I feel better in every way, and God has taken from me the desire for liquor. A new power has taken possession of me since Christ came into my life. Sir," he concluded, "if what you say is true, then how do you explain me? What God has done in me?"

The lecturer quickly slipped away from the scene, for he had no explanation to offer. That miner sent people home hearing the truth that the Bible is still the Word of the living God, that Jesus Christ is more than a myth, and that the gospel is the power of God unto salvation to every one that believeth.

Have you noticed how often Jesus silenced His enemies by asking a simple question or making a brief declaration? When He spoke one word of wisdom at the appropriate time, it exposed a thousand foolish ideas! Everyone stood speechless before Jesus!

FATHER, I'd like to join that miner in asking, "How do you explain me?" There is this difference. The miner was a down-and-outer who needed to be lifted; I was an up-and-outer who needed to be brought low. Both of us needed Gods saving grace to give us something we did not deserve, and God's mercy— to not give us what we did deserve. Thank You, Father, for giving Jesus!

For we ourselves also were sometimes foolish, disobedient, deceived, serving divers lust and pleasures, living in malice and envy, hateful, and hating one another. But after that the kindness and love of God, our Savior toward man appeared, not by works of righteousness which we have done, but according to his mercy he saved us by the WASHING OF REGENERATION, and the renewing of the Holy Spirit....being justified by his grace, we should be made heirs according to the hope of eternal life. (Titus: 3:3-7)

My Sudden Awakening

JAMIE JETT

explains... I RELUCTANTLY forced myself out of bed and into the shower at my dormitory. That Sunday morning, my boyfriend Nick and I were to drive an hour from Bethany College to Junction City where my father pastors a church. My parents were to take us out for lunch with a pastor friend of my father.

As I tried to wake up under the cool spray, I didn't give much thought to what the day would bring. I was mainly dreading the hassle of the long drive ahead. I had no inkling that a single conversation a few hours later would have such an impact on me.

That afternoon, Nick and I joined my parents and their guest, Joe Tosini, around a table at a Chinese restaurant. Sipping tea and clicking chopsticks, we relaxed and began to get acquainted.

Joe learned we were both Spirit-filled Christians and successful college students; the kind of kids, I thought, that make parents proud. The table conversation was going smoothly, and we were all enjoying ourselves when Pastor Tosini asked Nick and me the typical question adults pose to college students: "Tell me, what are you going to do with your life?"

We responded with the standard answers. Nick said he wanted to get a job in his field, exercise physiology. I mumbled something about law school, then ended up admitting I really didn't know. It was then that the easy-going chatter ended.

"You know," he said, "these answers really disappoint me." Silence blanketed the table as we stared at our guest, waiting for an explanation.

"Those answers not only bother me," he continued, "they anger me." It seemed like hours went by. At least I know enough time passed for me to experience a multitude of emotions.

"He doesn't even know me!" I thought. "Who is this guy anyway?" My feelings ranged from embarrassment to anger. Finally, I just told myself to calm down. My racing thoughts were halted as our guest spoke again.

"Is this what we're producing?" he asked my father. "Is our goal to raise nice children who don't sin, good citizens who will grow up and have nice houses?"

164

"Hey, that's not too bad these days." I thought to myself. "My mom seems pretty relieved!"

Joe continued by telling us about another college student he knows who isn't a Christian. "If she were sitting here," he said, "she'd answer those questions in exactly the same way. She's got career ambitions. She's not living immorally. The main difference between your life-style and hers is what you do on Sundays."

Then Nick came to our aid. "What should I have said?"

A huge smile crossed our guest's face. "I'm glad you asked," he said. "You should have said with fire in your eyes, 'I have a sure direction for my life. I'm going to join myself with people who have a heavenly vision to build God's church. If I'm an exercise physiologist or a lawyer, that'll be fine. But every dollar I make, every talent I possess, and everything God puts in my care will be used to live out my heavenly calling.'"

Joe said he was recruiting people just as the Marines do. He insisted he wanted to enlist young people who want their lives to be consumed with what God wants to accomplish for Himself.

Our answers had told him that our focus was on ourselves, our occupations. We needed to see God's vision, what He is doing. The important thing is not the role we play, but the entire production.

I let all of this sink in slowly. Our guest had observed that we were part of a generation anxiously waiting for something for which to give our lives. He was right. It fit!

I began thinking about my generation. Thanks to technology, we have more time than any generation to devote to the building of God's kingdom. We have vast resources. We're blessed with the conviction that God wants His church to rise up and become a people of praise and integrity. It was then I understood our guest's frustration when he heard me say, "I don't really know what I want to do with my life."

Some soul-searching began that day and I decided a change of thinking was definitely in order. What am I going to do with my life?

Now I am getting some answers. I can say confidently that God has put me in college to gain the skills He needs for me to help build His church. No matter what the future holds, I 'm going to join a group of people determined to do something of eternal value with their God-given talents. Whether I am a lawyer, a florist, or a mother of two or ten, I'm going to hold nothing back as I live to fulfill my heavenly vision. (J.J.)

What did He do with me...?
He set me apart for Himself!
Therefore, I am not my own...!

This whole question takes on new clarity when we go back to consider His sanctifying work when Jesus died on the Cross. Once we understand that as Jesus died on the Cross, we died with him—that is, we were crucified there with Him, when He was buried in the tomb, we were buried with Him, when He arose from the grave, we arose with Him—to a new position.

From that moment on we are separated from our old world and separated unto Him. In this separation, which is called sanctification we no longer belong to ourselves; our whole life is now to be ordered by Him for fulfilling His purpose.

Really, the question is not what am I going to do with my life, but what does He want to do with me, and through me. The Apostle Paul sums it up this way:

With eyes wide open to the mercies of God, I beg you, my brothers, as an act of intelligent worship, to give Him your bodies, as a living sacrifice, consecrated to Him and acceptable to Him.

Don't let the world around you squeeze you into its own mold, but let God remold your minds from within, so that you may prove in practice that the Plan of God for you is good, meets all His demands and moves toward the goal of true maturity. (Rom.12:1-2 Phillips Tr.)

FATHER, my heart responds with singing:

**Not what I wish to be, nor where I wish to go,
for who am I, that I should choose my way,
The Lord will choose for me,
I know tis better far,
so let me go or stay.**

The Love of the Father

(AUTHOR UNKNOWN). . .

SOME YEARS BACK when I was passing through a time of prolonged illness and the weakened physical condition which follows, I became vulnerable to Satan's attacks and his lying insinuations. At such a time, doubts and fears pressed in to almost overwhelm me. I lacked real peace. In my downcast condition I was especially concerned about my seeming lack of love, and my coldness of heart toward God appalled me!

It was when I picked up a DAILY BREAD and read the Monday devotional that I discovered this most precious gem of advice given to a fellow believer:

"When I go home, I expect to take up my baby girl on my knee, look into her sweet, trusting eyes, and listen to her delightful chatter. I'll do this because I thoroughly love that child.

"She's just a small girl, and she loves me very little. If my heart were breaking, her innocent sleep would not be disturbed. If my body racked with pain, her play would not be interrupted. Even if I were to die, she'd probably forget me in a few days.

"But all the money in the world could not buy my little daughter. And why? Does she love me, or do I love her? Do I withhold my love until I know she feels the same toward me? Certainly not! I love her because she's my child. She is very precious in my sight!

"Suddenly it dawned on me. In a new way I realized what the Father's love really meant. With tearful eyes, I could only exclaim: I see! It's not my love for God, but His love for me... that I should be thinking of.' And with that knowledge came a love for Him as never before. Then I realized why John had written: *"Herein is love, not that we loved God, but that He loved us."* And again: *"...we have known and believed the love that God hath to us."* (I John 4:10,16)

In this light, our problems look so different. This little daughter's heart was wholly pre-occupied with "her little world of interests." As long as she is a child her attention will be on herself, and there will be no room for anything else. It is exactly so with us.

THE FATHER'S LOVE	
	for ME
MY LOVE for GOD	1 John 3:1
1 Peter 1:8	

Perhaps this is the reason John warns us *"Love not the world, neither the things that are in the world. If any man love the world the love of the Father is not in him."*

FATHER, I begin to realize You love Your children, not only for who they are, but because of Who You are! From the beginning in Genesis we see a pattern of Your giving and... giving. And You enlightened Amy Carmichael to write "You can give without loving, but you cannot love without giving."

But...There is God

HANNAH WHITEHALL SMITH WRITES. . .
THERE WAS A TIME in my Christian life when I was passing through a great deal of questioning and perplexity. I felt that no Christian had ever had such peculiar difficulties as mine. There happened to be staying near me for a few weeks a lady who was considered to be a deeply spiritual Christian. I summoned up my courage one afternoon and went to see her. I poured out my troubles to her, expecting that she would take a deep interest in me and would do all she could to help me.

She listened patiently enough and did not interrupt me. But when I had finished my story and paused, expecting sympathy, she simply said, "Yes, all you say may be true, but then, in spite of it all, there is God."

"But," I continued, "surely you did not understand how very serious and perplexing my difficulties are."

"Oh yes, I did," replied my friend, "but then, as I tell you, there is God."

I could not induce her to make any other answer. It seemed to me most disappointing and unsatisfactory. I felt that my peculiar and difficult experiences could not be met by anything so simple as the statement, "Yes, but there is God." I knew God was there, of course, but I felt I needed something more than just God. I came to the conclusion that my friend, for all her great reputation as a spiritual teacher, was at any rate not able to handle my problems.

My need was so great, however, that I did not give up with my first attempt. I went to her again and again, always with the hope that she would sometime begin to understand the importance of my difficulties and would give me adequate help. It was of no use. I was never able to draw forth any other answer. Always, to everything. would come the simple reply, "Yes, I know; but there is always God."

At last, by power of her continual repetition, I became convinced that my friend truly believed that the mere fact of the existence of God, as the Creator and Redeemer of mankind, and of me as a member of the race, was an all-sufficient answer to every possible need. She said it so often and seemed so sure that I began to wonder whether God might be enough, even for my overwhelming and peculiar need. From wondering I came gradually to believing that, since He is my Creator and Redeemer, He must be enough. A conviction burst upon me that He truly was enough. My eyes were opened to the absolute and utter all-sufficiency of God.

My troubles disappeared, and I wondered how I could ever have been such an idiot as to be troubled by them, when all the while there was God. The Almighty and All-seeing God, the God who had created me, was on my side and eager to care for me and help me. Yes, I had found out that God was enough, and my soul was at rest. (HWS)

FATHER, I remember when Job needed counsel, a friend came with this advice: *"Acquaint now thyself with him, and be at peace: thereby good shall come unto thee. Receive, I pray thee, the law from His mouth, and lay up His words in thine heart."* **(Job 20:21-22)**

A Calendar Speaks

DICK HILLIS SPEAKS. . .
OF GOD'S SPECIAL PROVISION. As founder of Overseas Crusades, Dick served in China with his late wife Margaret. In this story, he reminisces about their war-threatened mission compound and God's provision for his family.

It was January 15, 1941. The invading Japanese army was only a few miles from our mission station in Central China. My wife Margaret was alone in the compound. The previous day I had become suddenly ill and was taken by rickshaw to the hospital 115 miles away.

Unexpectedly, on that very day the commanding officer of the defending Nationalist troops entered briskly.

"The enemy is advancing," the Colonel announced, "and we have orders not to defend this city. For your own safety, you should find refuge in one of the villages away from the city."

As the Colonel departed, the icy January wind swept through the small room. Suddenly, the enormity of her danger over-whelmed Margaret. She was alone in a war-threatened Chinese village, totally responsible for the safety of our two children—one-year old Johnny and two-month old Margaret Anne. When Margaret looked at the little daily Scripture calendar on the wall, she realized I couldn't return until mid-February.

"How can I ever manage without my husband?" she thought. "The decisions I make may determine the life or death of my babies."

Margaret later admitted she had not yet experienced the full wonder of God's sufficiency and power to guide when all else failed. Nor could she realize how He would use something as prosaic as a calendar on a kitchen wall to be that guide.

By mid-afternoon, the soldiers' departure created panic. Families packed their goods and fled. The church elders called on Margaret before they left. "Come with us," they pleaded. "We will care for you while Pastor Hillis is away."

Margaret looked at the concern in their eyes. She loved these people, but knew their village huts held death for Western babies. Many tiny graves in our mission compound proved this danger.

Yet how could she explain this without offense: that she should not take their own children into the unheated, mud-floored huts where three and four generations crowded together? Just a few weeks earlier, a six-month old son of the nearest American family had died of the dreaded dysentery.

No, her babies would stay near her own kitchen where she could boil milk and water and where one room was always kept warm.

Margaret thanked the village Christians for their concern, but said she'd wait for her husband's return and watch over the mission property. That night she went to bed shaking with fear. "Would the hardened soldiers of the imperial army attack during the night?" she wondered.

Little Johnny awoke whimpering in the cold. Taking him into bed with her, Margaret lay awake a long time. Listening to the wind rattling the waxed-paper window panes, she prayed that her little boy would live to see his daddy again.

Early the next morning, she hurried to the kitchen to start the water boiling for Margaret Anne's bottle. Intuitively, she reached up to the wall-calendar and tore off yesterday's date. The Scripture verse for the new day gleamed like sunlight.

"What time I am afraid, I will trust in Thee" (Psalm 56:3).

"Well, I certainly am afraid," Margaret admitted to herself. "I fulfill that part of the verse! **Now** indeed is the time to trust God."

Somehow God's promise sustained her through that tense day.

The city was being evacuated rapidly. Other church members came to invite Margaret to their country huts. But that Scripture held the young mother. She was not to panic, but to trust. Then the compound gatekeeper came to Margaret, his eyes blurred with fear. "I must leave," he said. "Please, pastor's wife. Please, come take refuge with me in my village beyond the city."

Margaret hesitated. The deserted city would be an open invitation to bandits and looters. What would she do without the protection of the gatekeeper? But the risk to her babies in the village huts was certain. In the city she faced only unknown fears. She declined the gatekeeper's offer and watched him as he apologetically left her.

It was noon before Margaret remembered to pull the page off the little daily calendar on the wall. The Scripture for the day read—

*"And they that know Thy name will put their trust in Thee, for
Thou Lord, hast not forsaken them that seek Thee"* (Psalm 9:10).

As Margaret bowed her head over the noon meal, she poured
out her gratitude to God for those particular words for the
moment.

Her main concern now was food. All the shops in town were
boarded up. Although the goats that provided the babies' milk
were still in the compound, the man who milked them had left the
village. Tomorrow Margaret would have to milk them herself.
She wondered if she could ever make the balky little beasts hold
still.

Margaret slept uneasily that night. Worrying about how she
would feed her children, she was only sure of one thing: that she
should stay in the city and, somehow, trust God.

The next morning, she was awakened by the sound of distant
gunfire. The Japanese must be advancing toward the city. She
knew she must milk the goats before the actual shelling of the city
began, making the goats frightened and unmanageable.

She decided before she faced those goats, she had better fortify
herself with a bowl of rice gruel and with the new day's
Scripture promise. She tore the old page from the calendar and
today God's Word to her was—

"I will nourish you, and your little ones" (Genesis 50:21).

The timeliness of these daily verses was becoming almost
uncanny. With some curiosity Margaret examined the back of the
calendar pad. It had been put together in England the year
before. But God in His all-knowing love had provided the very
words she needed a year later—on the other side of the world.

Margaret was still eating the gruel when a woman suddenly
stepped into the kitchen, carrying a pail of steaming goat's milk.

"May I stay and help you?" she asked, holding up the pail.
"See, I have milked your goats." Diminutive Mrs. Lee had been
our neighbor for years, but that morning Margaret felt that she
had been sent from heaven. Mrs. Lee explained that she had no
family currently living and that she wished to show her gratitude
to the mission by staying in the city with Margaret.

Abruptly, late in the day, a loud rapping at the gate set the
women's heart pounding. Her face beaming, Mrs. Lee opened the

door and ushered in the caller. A frail, black-robed country woman came in with a live chicken and a basket of eggs.

"Peace, peace," she said, giving the customary Christian greeting.

Terrifying noise of the cannons had not kept her away when she remembered the missionaries would be hungry. God had fulfilled the promise on the calendar. He had seen to it that the little ones were nourished.

That night Margaret's heart was full of hope. While shells burst over the city, she prayed that somehow God would spare these gentle people we loved.

Next morning, Margaret rushed down to the little square of paper hanging on its nail and tore off another page—

"When I cry unto Thee, then shall mine enemies turn back: this I know; for God is for me" (Psalm 56:9).

"Was it too much to believe it this time?" Margaret pondered. "Surely it couldn't be right to take literally a verse chosen 'just by chance' from an English calendar?"

As the gunfire drew closer, Margaret and Mrs. Lee began to prepare the house for an invasion. Any papers that might possibly be construed to have military significance had to be hidden or destroyed, so they searched her desk and the church buildings and burned papers that might be misunderstood.

By nightfall, the gunfire sounded from both sides of the city. The women went to bed dressed, prepared at any moment to meet the Japanese invaders.

Margaret woke abruptly in the early dawn and strained her ears for the crunch of military boots on gravel. But only a deep stillness surrounded her. Misgivings mixed with excitement as Margaret and Mrs. Lee went to the gatehouse, each carrying a child. Mrs. Lee was the first to stick out a cautious head.

"There's no one in the street," she told Margaret. "Shall we go out?"

The women stepped through the gate and watched as the streets began to fill, not with Japanese soldiers, but with townspeople returning from their country hiding places. Had the Chinese won? As if in answer to the unspoken question, the Colonel stepped up. "Pastor's wife," he said with relief, "I have been concerned about you!"

Then he told Margaret that the Japanese had withdrawn. No, they had not been defeated. Nor could anyone arrive at a reasonable conjecture concerning their retreat. The enemy had simply turned back.

Margaret, stepping into her kitchen with eyes fixed on a little block of paper pinned to the wall, sent silent thanksgiving to the God Who is enough.

"You could say it was just a calendar," she said later. "You could say that strangers had chosen those verses without any thought of China, or of the war that would be raging when those dates fell due. But to me, it was more than a calendar. No stranger had picked those lines. To me, it was the handwriting of God." (D.H.)

How many times we have read about this in His word, or heard others testify about our Father's faithfulness. Yet it is only when we have personally experienced His supply—as Margaret did—that we can join these writers in exalting God's faithfulness:

"Great is Thy faithfulness..." (Lamentations 3:23).

"Who is a strong Lord like unto Thee? or to Thy faithfulness round about Thee?" (Psalm 89:8).

"My loving kindness will I not take from him, nor suffer My faithfulness to fail" (Psalm 89:33).

"Thou hast done wonderful things; Thy counsels of old are faithfulness and truth" (Isaiah 25:1).

David continues: *"I know, O Lord, that Your laws are righteous, and in faithfulness You have afflicted me. May Your unfailing love be my comfort, according to Your promise to Your servant"* (Psalm 119:75-76 NIV).

Is there any other way to learn faithfulness—besides afflictions? Someone has said we can learn *conceptually*, but we must also learn *circumstantially*. All of Your servants seem to have discovered this.

FATHER, I am sure if there was any easier way to learn some lessons, we could expect You to use them. Today I will be content to allow You to do what is best for me... and for Your plans.

The Song the Lepers Loved

A Native Pastor Took. . . his foreign friend to visit a large leper colony in Africa. When they entered the colony, they had to put on sterile robes and medicated boots as they walked past the little houses and gardens to their great temple. Permission had been granted to hold a service for the Christians. One by one the sufferers came limping into the gathering. Their swollen faces wore smiles and their hearts seemed full of joy.

When the lepers had reached their places, the leader asked, What is your most loved hymn? The foreign visitor imagined those lepers would call for "I Must Tell Jesus All of My Troubles." To his surprise, the song the lepers chose was:

"A Singing I go along life's road,
Praising the Lord, praising the Lord:
Singing I go along life's road,
For Jesus has lifted my load!"

Were these lepers *victims* imprisoned in sorrowful conditions? No, they were *victors*, announcing their joyous captivity to the Lord. To us it seems incredible!

Yet the most joyous book in the Bible comes from the pen of an author chained to a Roman guard. Many scholars are convinced the Apostle Paul wrote Philippians from a Roman cell just about the time Nero began tossing Christians to the ravenous lions and burning them as torches to illuminate his banquets. How could a rational man devote a letter to the topic of joy while his survival was in serious jeopardy? It seems impossible, *but God!*

You may recall that many years earlier, when that church was birthing, Paul and Silas had been in prison. During the night hours as they rejoiced in singing, God responded with an earthquake that shook their cell doors open. The jailer was converted! The *unpredictable* happened *because a sovereign God* was working out His purpose for the Philippian church. Out of personal experience Paul could write: *"Therefore, my brethren, dearly beloved and longed for, MY JOY AND CROWN, so stand fast in the Lord... Rejoice in the Lord always and again I say rejoice"* (Phil. 4:1,4).

In Philippians Paul uses the word *'joy'* or *'rejoice'* every few paragraphs. It is not *where* you are, but *what* you are that determines your joy.

176

I can still recall an evening many years ago when I was visiting a church in the Queens, NY. A letter had just arrived from China. A sister of Watchman Nee had sent the personal letter which Nee had written to her shortly before his death. Those who read it explained the characters were strong, as was the tone of the few words he wrote: "I have learned how to maintain my joy."

How often in following days when a cloud would pass over my spirit, have I remembered that Nee had been in prison more than 20 years at that time. While he was frail in body, yet he was rejoicing in spirit. He had learned the secret of maintaining the joy of the Lord.

Joy or depression—it is always my choice. Each day I can choose to send my roots into Your river of grace, and joy will be my expression. I see then that the secret for maintaining my daily joy is my choice.

Life may seem hard, BUT GOD is so good and merciful,
Life may seem unfair, BUT GOD is just and loving.
Life may seem unpredictable, BUT GOD is so sovereign,
Life may seem temporary, BUT GOD is eternal.

This helps me to recognize that holding the right perspective makes the difference. If I look at what I may be facing today, I will succumb to depression. Only as I look beyond today to see what God has planned in eternity, can I say: "Joy Unspeakable and Full of Glory."

Today you are making this choice: Be miserable, depressed, and live under the circumstances, and the atmosphere around you will not only surround you but others. Or, you can choose to be joyous—even contagious—for others will catch your joy. I realize that Jesus was a man of sorrows Who was acquainted with grief because of the conditions around Him. But I am also convinced He lived in the long- range perspective:

"For the joy set before Him, He endured the cross."

Jesus looked down the corridor of time to see what would please His Father, and He ignored the temporal to live for the eternal.

FATHER, only by Your grace can I make this same choice. Joy will be my atmosphere today, and I'll join the lepers in their song:

SINGING I GO ALONG LIFE'S ROAD,
For Jesus has lifted my load.

Unfolding The Will of God. . .

AFTER FIFTY YEARS of observing how Christians fulfill their calling, I am convinced with this principle: Usually, the will of God for our lives is not found by searching, but by allowing Him to unfold His will as we respond to the circumstances in which we are placed in.

A beautiful young girl in India was about to be married. All eyes admired this capable young Christian as she was preparing for her marriage.

Suddenly, sores appeared on her hands. Everyone was shocked to discover it was leprosy. Instead of moving to her lover and the home they had planned, she moved into a leper asylum. Instead of a wedding, she slowly walked with her brother into the dreaded place that was to become her home.

What disappointment filled her heart! All around her were women—wretched, dirty, despairing, having faces without hope. When she saw them, she threw her head on her brother's shoulder, and wept.

"My God," she sobbed, "am I going to become as they are?

She was so overwhelmed, those about her feared she might jump into the well to end it all.

One day, missionaries who sympathized with her asked if she would like to be a help to those poor women.

It was as though God sent a special ray of hope to her. She caught the vision. Purpose and meaning gripped her as she turned from her self-pity. She started a school and taught the women to read, write, and sing. Since she could play music, a folding organ was brought by her missionary friends. Gradually, a transformation took place in the facility. Their houses were made clean, neat, and tidy. The women began to wash their clothes and comb their hair. That once horrible place became a place of blessing.

After some years passed, she gave this testimony: "When I first came to the asylum, I doubted whether there was a God. Now, I know that God had a work for me to do. If I had not become a leper, I never would have discovered my work. Every day I live, I thank Him, because He has given me this work to do."

Did God arrange this tragedy for her life? Surely not! But He knows how to turn the consequences from past generations of sin to work for His glory. It was not her searching for God's will, but rather that she allowed Him to <u>unfold</u> His will in her life through her circumstances. The One Whom this world would accuse of imposing a "frowning providence" upon her, turns out to be Our loving Father.

God's Word speaks: *"O the depth of the riches both of the wisdom and knowledge of God! How unsearchable are his judgments, and **His ways past finding out**! For who hath known the mind of the Lord? Or who hath been His counselor?"* (Rom. 11:33-34).

My heart responds: "Father, I am so glad You do not expect me to understand your ways, but simply to trust You. What I have already learned of You is that Your wisdom transcends all my reasonings."

Cleaning up Corruption

A YOUNG PASTOR MOVED. . .
to a city of 25,000 to assume the duties of a church. Shortly after arriving, some of his church leaders told him they thought he should attack the city administration, because the mayor, department chiefs, and the members of the council were corrupt and the city had a bad reputation in their state.

The pastor asked for time to pray for wisdom, then decided to request a ten-minute appointment with the mayor. During the appointment, after some general remarks, he said to the mayor:

"I want to congratulate you on the honor and responsibility that were laid on you when you were chosen mayor of this city. Yet I need to tell you that there could be a greater honor waiting for you, something far bigger than the office of a mayor of a city like this."

Assuming this stranger might represent some high-up politician, the mayor listened with evident interest. "You ought to be a servant of Jesus Christ... for there are great rewards for those who live for eternal values," said the young minister.

In astonishment the mayor said, "No one ever spoke to me like this before." Since the time for the appointment had ended, the minister left, but the next day the agitated voice of the mayor said to him over the phone, "Won't you come and talk with me? I have thought of what you said ever since you left. I must see you."

Two weeks later, not only did the mayor come into the pastor's church, but the chief of police, the chief of the fire department, and five aldermen—all yielded themselves to Christ. The city was cleaned up... in God's way.

It is one thing to boldly attack as a champion of righteousness; it is yet another to model the way of peace, mercy and grace, as this pastor chose to do.

When we observe our Lord Jesus, we discover that He chose to offer light first. Only after they rejected light and chose to rebel against it, would He begin confrontation.

FATHER, this world is so full of sin, darkness and rebellion we cannot predict how men will respond. Let me be wise, as this young pastor, and using Your methods become a peace-maker.

Learning the Way of Peace

(AUTHOR UNKNOWN)

AS I WAS WALKING across a bridge one day, and I saw a man standing on the edge about to jump off. So I ran over and said "Stop! Don't do it!" Why shouldn't I?" he asked.

I said, "Well there's so much to live for!"

He said, "Like what?"

I said, "Well, are you religious or atheist?"

He said, "Religious."

I said, "Me too! Are you Christian or Buddhist?"

He said, "Christian."

I said, "Me too! Are you Catholic or Protestant?"

He said, "Protestant."

I said, "Me too! Are you Episcopalian or Baptist?"

He said, "Baptist!"

I said, "Wow! Me too! Are you Baptist Church of God or Baptist Church of the Lord?"

He said, "Baptist Church of God!"

I said, "Me too! Are you Original Baptist Church of God, or are you Reformed Baptist Church of God?"

He said, "Reformed Baptist Church of God!"

I said, "Me too! Are you Reformed Baptist Church of God, Reformation of 1879, or Reformed Baptist Church of God, Reformation 1915?"

He said, "Reformed Baptist Church of God—1915!"

I said, "Die, you heretic!" and with disgust I pushed him off.

Of course you realize this is a manufactured parable, designed to emphasize the danger of developing a narrow mind-set that cannot agree with anyone. Let me quickly say, it is important to have convictions that are formed by the Word and the Spirit. And it is necessary to receive other believers even though we cannot agree with their interpretations. Frankly when I read this story, I wanted to push both of them off the bridge. But that would be my carnal reaction. Then I remembered: to react is to perpetuate the problem; but to act with God's wisdom (epi-gnosis) is to nurture the way of peace.

Many years ago I was conducting a series of meetings in a small church in Missouri. Sunday noon my associate and I were invited to a parish home for dinner. The lady of the house was most hospitable, and "religious." I had discerned from our conversation that she was "very strong" in some of her convictions.

As we at the table to eat, she announced, "I don't eat any meat, but I have fixed chicken for my husband and for you. You can make your choice!" I knew exactly what my partner, who was sitting next to the husband, would say: "Mame, please pass the chicken!" (I knew that he was seeking to gain some entrance into the heart of this alienated husband).

After we had bowed to offer "grace," I felt it was wisdom for me to keep open the door of this "needy wife." So I encouraged her by saying, "I am at liberty to eat or not eat chicken, but today I'll save the chicken for your husband." This gesture encouraged her to proceed with her convictions, and show me some booklets she had written.

I soon recognized she was not only strong but had sought to impose some extreme issues that had alienated her husband; but this also made her the local champion in their church. That she was sincere, devout and aggressive were most admirable qualities.

Later that afternoon when we were alone, I sought to explain what Paul meant by the "law of love concerning doubtful things."

I asked her, "Would you rather see your husband won to the Lord, or produce more booklets that champion your convictions?" I could see this question was really searching her heart motive. She was silent! She did love the Lord, and she wanted to walk pleasing to God.

She listened quietly as I read for several minutes from Romans:

So then every one of us shall give account of himself to God....
"...if thy brother be grieved with thy meat, now walkest thou not
charitably. Destroy not him with thy meat, for whom Christ died.
For the kingdom of God is not meat or drink, but righteousness,
peace and joy in the Holy Spirit... therefore follow after the things
which make for peace, and things wherewith one may edify another."

I wondered if any thing I had said about walking charitably toward her husband had registered in her heart. Would she build a bridge and seek the way of peace in their home? The following week we moved to a nearby church. I think she made the right choice, for I observed that her husband accompanied her to each of the meetings during that next week.

"For He is our peace, who hath made both one, and hath broken down the middle wall of partition between us; having abolished... the enmity..." (Eph 2:14)

Peace and Righteousness Kissed

WE HAVE USED TWO STORIES showing the unusual ministry of George Whitefield. Now let me introduce John Wesley, another much used preacher whose ministry greatly affected the history of the church in the eighteenth century. Both of these great men were mightily used of God, though they worked independently.

It had became a public shame that such spiritual giants in their early days of ministry separated because of theological differences. It is not our desire here to explore their differences, but to simply show how God worked in the heart of each because Whitefield and Wesley both recognized their need to love and their duty to win souls to Jesus Christ.

We will acknowledge that Whitefield's strong stand on election, and Wesley's deep conviction on sanctification forced them to work separately for many years. However, we can rejoice that in the sovereign dealing of God, along with each man reaching more wisdom and meekness, a measure of reconciliation finally came. In October 1741 Whitefield penned this personal letter to Wesley:

Though much may be said for my doing it, yet I am sorry.
Now that any such thing dropped from my pen and I
humbly ask pardon. I find I love you as much as ever and
pray, if it be His blessed will, that we be all united together...
May God remove all obstacles that now prevent our union!
In about three weeks I hope to be in Bristol. May all disputing
cease, and each of us talk of nothing but Jesus and Him
crucified. This is my resolution!

From our observation we can see the strong nature of Whitefield (righteousness) making room for peace; but we can also see the strong conviction of Wesley (peace) making room for righteousness. Yes, God was maneuvering behind the scenes, as He always does, for a couple months later the two men met in Bristol. In the time between Whitefield had married Elizabeth Delamotte, who happened to be a friend of John Wesley. When the two men met, George acknowledged his responsibility for the breakup of fellowship, and they agreed to love one another, even though they would continue to work separately.

Seven years later Wesley recorded his rejoicing in the way that God used Whitefield and also commented after hearing him preach, "How wise is God in giving different talents to different preachers!"

While it was not always so among his followers, Wesley never encouraged criticism of Whitefield. One small-minded disciple once asked, "Do you think we shall see Mr Whitefield in heaven?"

"No," Wesley replied, and the man looked pleased that he had aimed his flattery well.

"No sir," said Wesley, "I fear not. Mr Whitefield will be so near the Throne and we at such a distance, we shall hardly get sight of him."

In his great love chapter Paul reminds us: "Now... we see as through a glass darkly." We see in part, but in that glorious day when we shall see clearly—we shall be glad then, that we made a deliberate choice not to falsely accuse one another but to guard our tongues. Even when we disagree in a vital principle, as Paul did with Peter, we will keep our spirit right and our heart full of love. Those things that are right(eous) must also have the kiss of peace.

FATHER, help me to hold my peace, when I would be quick to adjust spiritual issues that need correction. Just as You had your timing for the reconciliation of Whitefield and Wesley, so I can await Your timing to reconcile me with those who have different convictions. Could it be there is someone reading this who has a propensity to aloofness toward those who disagree; please give them a special measure of grace right now to become a peace-maker.

"Thou wilt keep him in perfect peace whose mind is steadfast, because he trusts in You." (Isa. 26:3)

Why the Firing Ceased

GOD IMPOSED HIS RIGHTEOUSNESS. . . A day was dawning on a battlefield in Northern France through a fog so thick that no one could see more than a few yards from the trenches. During the night the Germans had drawn back their lines a little, while the French had advanced a little. Now between the two positions a lonely farmhouse was still standing. As the sun rose, heavy guns began to boom.

Then suddenly the firing on both sides ceased, and there fell a strange, dead stillness. Midway between the trenches, near the shattered farmhouse, they saw what seemed impossible! But it was not. There in the green meadow, crawling on his hands and knees, was a little child. He appeared perfectly happy and contented. In fact, the child's laughter was heard as he clutched a dandelion.

Not a shot was fired from either line. Scarcely did any soldier on either side dare to breathe. This spot had been an inferno of shots and shells. Now it was something like a peaceful island. Where did this crawling child come from? How did he get there?

Suddenly, a soldier jumped out of his trench and ran to where the child was crawling. He tenderly took him up and carried him back to shelter. No shots came from either trenches, but instead from both lines there rang out a mighty cheer. In the midst of sudden peace, a moment of righteousness was reigning. The entrance of a little child had brought peace; yes, it was just like two thousand years ago, when the Prince of Peace was born on that first Christmas morning.

From God's viewpoint, we see a larger window: When God intervenes in the affairs of men, it is not to take sides among men. Usually, both sides are convinced they are right. But God's way is to demonstrate there is an even higher "rightness" which transcends the reasonings of men.

In the gospel this is demonstrated when an offended brother pleads with Jesus to judge his case, that he might receive his rightful portion of the inheritance. Jesus refused! Why? No doubt because He saw the same greed in the hearts of each of the brothers.

Often you hear children shouting. One says, "but I'm right," and the other responds, "but I'm right." Whether among warring nations, or among fussing individuals God refuses to take sides. It is because His way is to penetrate much deeper—to deal with the "I'm right" spirit.

Usually Jesus is saying to all of us, "you're both wrong—and you'll never understand why I'm right until you learn to understand principles from my viewpoint."

"It is unthinkable that God would do wrong, that the Almighty would pervert justice" (Job 34:12 NIV).

"He will judge the world in righteousness; He will govern the peoples with justice." (Ps. 9:8 NIV).

"Righteousness and justice are the foundation of Your throne; love and faithfulness go before You" (Ps. 89:14 NIV).

FATHER, I would have loved to sing with the heavenly host that Christmas morning, who were praising God and saying: "Glory to God in the highest, and on earth peace, good will toward men." I do realize that kind of peace must begin within me. Only then can Your peace flow through me to others: I choose today to become a peace-maker in my small circle.

Their Joy Was Missing

WATCHMAN NEE EXPLAINS. . .

I RECALL A STORY of two brothers who both cultivated paddy fields. Their fields were halfway up the hill; others were lower down. In the great heat, they drew water by day and went to sleep at night. One night, while they were sleeping, the farmers lower down the hill dug a hole in the irrigation channel surrounding the brother's fields and let all the water flow down on their own fields.

The next morning the brothers saw what had happened, but said nothing. They filled the troughs with water, and again all the water was drawn off the following night. Still they uttered no word of protest when they discovered the mean trick the same farmers had played on them. It seemed so unfair, yet they were Christians. Ought not Christians to be patient?

This game was repeated seven nights in succession; and for seven days these two brothers silently suffered the wrong. Quietly they continued doing what was good and right. We would assume that Christians who could allow themselves to be treated like this day after day, and never utter a word of reproach, would surely be overflowing with joy.

Strange to say, they were not happy at all, and their unhappiness distressed them to such an extent that they brought the matter to a brother who was in the Lord's service. Having stated their case, they asked him: How does it come about that, having suffered all this wrong for a full week, we are still unhappy?

This brother had some experience and he replied: You are unhappy because you have not gone the full length. You should first irrigate those farmers' fields and then irrigate your own. You go back and test it out, and see whether or not your hearts find rest. They agreed to try, and off they went.

Next morning they were afoot earlier than ever, and their first business was to irrigate the fields of those farmers who had so persistently robbed their fields of water. And this amazing thing happened—the more they labored watering their persecutors' land, the happier they became. By the time they had finished watering their own land their hearts were at perfect rest. When the brothers repeated this for two or three days, the offending farmers called to apologize and added: If this is Christianity, then we want to hear more about it.

Let us consider what had happened. At the first those two brothers had been most patient for days; was that not right? They had labored in the intense heat to irrigate their paddy fields and, without a word of complaint, had allowed others to steal their water—was that not very good? What then was lacking that they had no joy?

It is important that we recognize two very different kingdoms— the moral kingdom of natural reasoning, and the spiritual kingdom in which the way of divine Life operates.

In the moral kingdom, when men do what is good and right, it will bring temporary peace. However, in the spiritual kingdom, we must go beyond what is good and right to sacrifice ourselves, (the brothers did this when they watered their neighbor's fields first): In this *God was satisfied* and He gave them great joy.

This will help us to understand why Paul wrote to the Romans:

"God's kingdom... is not meat or drink, but righteousness, peace and JOY in the Holy Ghost." It is His joy that makes the difference!

FATHER, I realize I have been content too often with the moral kingdom of righteousness and peace. Now, I recognize if I would move beyond the moral kingdom of men to live in Your spiritual kingdom..., (then) I must seek that first. It is Your guarantee: You will add much JOY. I can understand why Jesus encouraged us to "seek first the kingdom of God... and all these things will be added."

Fulfilling God's Will Involves

THE END	THE PROCESS	THE TIMING
(God's goal)	(His ways)	(When)
Eph. 1:9-11	Rom. 11:33	Luke 19:44
James 5:11	Psalm 86:11	Rom. 9:9
Eph. 3:9-11	2 Sam. 22:31	1 Peter 1: 5, 9

EVEN A MOST casual look at God's dealing with men in the Bible will reveal how God's will involves three things: His goal, His process and His timing. Those special individuals who had a glimpse of His glorious End, but needed to patiently wait for fulfillment suffered the trial of their faith. Consider God's promise to Abraham (the pattern man) that he would have a two-fold family numbering as the sands of the seashore and the stars in the sky. That promise seemed most incredible, yet from our enlarged window we can now begin to recognize how that goal will one day be accomplished in the new heaven and earth. (Abraham judged Him faithful who had promised, and must we.)

It was this great burden of the Apostle Paul that all men should see and appreciate the grand finale, i.e. the ultimate purpose (telios) of Father/God for Himself, and for His family:

When I think of the greatness of this great Plan, I fall on my knees before God, the Father (from Whom all fatherhood, earthly and heavenly, derives its name...). (Phillips Tr. Eph. 3:14)

God's Ways (Process) Unfolds

The Matchless Pearl

A HEAVY SPLASH. . .
was followed by many ripples, and then the water below the pier
was still. An American missionary watched intently from the low
Indian pier, his eyes riveted on the place where a stream of little
bubbles rose to the surface from deep under the water. Suddenly
a black head appeared, and a pair of bright eyes looked up. Then
he watched the old Indian pearl diver clamber onto the dock.

"As nice a dive as I've ever seen, Rambhau!" cried David
Morse, the missionary.

"Look at this one, Sahib," said Rambhau, taking a big oyster
from between his teeth. "I think it'll be good."

Morse took it and while he was prying it open with his pocket
knife, Rambhau was pulling other small oysters from his loin-
cloth.

"Rambhau! Look!" exclaimed Morse, "This is a treasure!"

"Yes, a good one," shrugged the diver.

"Good! Have you ever seen a better pearl? It's perfect, isn't it!"
Morse had been turning the big pearl over and over and then
handed it to his Indian friend.

"Oh, but there are better pearls, much better. Why, I have
one"—his voice trailed off. "See this one—has imperfections, the
black specks here, this tiny dent... even in shape it is a bit oblong,
but good as pearls go. I remember you say of your God, that people look perfect to themselves, but God sees them as they actually
are."

In a few minutes the two men started up the dusty road to town.

"You're right, Rambhau. God does offer a perfect righteousness to all who will simply believe and accept his free offer of salvation through His Beloved Son."

"But, Sahib, as so many times before I have told you, it's too
easy. I cannot accept that. Perhaps I am too proud. I must work
for my place in heaven."

"Oh Rambhau! Don't you see, you'll never get to heaven that
way. There's only one way to heaven. And see, Rambhau, you are
getting older now. Perhaps this is your last season of diving for
pearls. If you ever want to see heaven's gates of pearl, you must
accept the new life God offers you in His Son."

"My last season! Yes, you are right. Today was my last day of diving. This is the last month of the year, and I have many preparations yet to make."

"You should prepare for the life to come."

"That's just what I'm going to do. Do you see that man over there? He is a pilgrim, perhaps to Bombay or Calcutta. He walks barefooted and picks the sharpest stones... and see... every few rods he kneels down and kisses the road. That is good! The first day of the New Year, I will begin my pilgrimage. All my life I have planned it. I shall make sure of heaven this time. I am planning to go to Delhi on my knees."

"Man! You're crazy! It's nine hundred miles to Delhi! The skin will break on your knees, and you'll have blood poisoning or leprosy long before you get to Bombay."

"No, I must get to Delhi. And then the immortals will regard me. The suffering will be sweet, for it will purchase heaven for me."

"Rambhau! My friend! You can't! How can you let yourself do this when Jesus Christ has died to purchase heaven for you?"

But the old man could not be moved. He was set in his ways. "You are my dearest friend on earth, Sahib Morse. Through all these years you have stood beside me. In sickness and want, you have been sometimes my only friend. But even you cannot turn me from this great desire to purchase eternal bliss. I must go to Delhi."

It seemed so useless to argue. The old pearl diver could not understand, nor could he accept that salvation was a free gift.

That afternoon a while later, Morse answered a knock at the door.

"My good friend!" cried Morse. "Come in, Rambhau."

"No," said the pearl diver, "I want you to come with me to my house. Please, Sahib, for a short time. I have something to show you. Please do not say, 'No.'"

The heart of the missionary leaped. Perhaps God was answering prayer at last. "Of course, I'll come," he said.

"I will leave for Delhi just one week from today," said Rambhau as they neared his house ten minutes later. The missionary's heart sank. Morse took a seat on the chair his friend had built especially for him, where many times he had explained to the diver God's way to heaven. Almost immediately Rambhau left the room to return with a small but heavy English strong box.

"I have had this box for years," he said. "I keep only one thing in it. Now I will tell you about it. Sahib Morse, I once had a son."

"A son! Why, Rambhau, you had never said a word about him!"

"No, Sahib, I couldn't." Even as he spoke the diver's eyes were moistened. "Now, I must tell you, for soon I will leave, and who knows whether I shall ever return? My son was a diver, too. He was the best pearl diver on the coast of India. He had the swiftest dive, the keenest eye, the strongest arm, the longest breath of any man who sought for pearls. What joy he brought me.

"He always dreamed of finding a pearl beyond all that had ever been found. One day he found it! But in finding it he was under water too long. He lost his life soon after."

The old pearl diver bowed his head and for a moment his whole body shook. "All these years I have kept the pearl," he continued, "but now I am going, never to return... and to you, my best friend, I am giving my pearl."

The old man worked the combination on the strong box and drew from it a carefully wrapped package. Gently opening the cotton, he picked up a mammoth pearl and placed it in the hand of the missionary. It was one of the largest pearls ever found off the coast of India, and it glowed with a luster and brilliance never seen in cultured pearls. It would have brought a fabulous sum in any market.

The missionary was speechless and gazed with awe. "Rambhau," he said, "this is a wonderful pearl, an amazing pearl. Let me buy it. I would give ten thousand rupees for it."

"Sahib, said Rambhau, stiffening his whole body, "this pearl is beyond all price. No man in all the world has money enough to pay what this pearl is worth to me. On the market a million rupees could not buy it."

"I will not sell it. You may only have it as a gift."

"No, Rambhau, I cannot accept that. As much as I want the pearl, I cannot accept it that way. Perhaps I am proud, but that is too easy. I must pay for it or work for it."

The old pearl diver was stunned. "You don't understand at all, Sahib. Don't you see? My only son gave his life to get this pearl, and I wouldn't sell it for money. Its worth is in the lifeblood of my son. I cannot sell this, but do permit me to give it to you. Just accept it in token of the love I bear for you."

The missionary was choked and for a moment could not speak. Then he gripped the hand of the old man.

"Rambhau," he said in a low voice. "Don't you see? That is exactly what you have been saying to God."

The old diver looked long and searchingly at the missionary... slowly he began to understand... light was breaking in.

"God is offering to you eternal life as a free gift. It is so great and priceless that no money on earth could buy it. No man on earth could earn it. No man is good enough to deserve it. It cost God the lifeblood of His only Son to produce an entrance for you into heaven. In a hundred pilgrimages, you could not earn that entrance. All you can do is accept it as a token of God's love for you, a sinner.

"Rambhau, of course, I will accept the pearl in deep humility, praying God I may be worthy of your love. Now, Rambhau, won't you too accept God's great gift of eternal life, in deep humility, knowing it cost Him the death of His Son to offer it to you? Please accept! *'The gift of God is eternal life through Jesus Christ our Lord.'*"

Great tears were rolling down the cheeks of the old man. The veil was lifting. At last he understood!

"Sahib, I see it! I do believe Jesus gave Himself for me. I accept Him... *Thanks be unto God for His unspeakable gift"* (II Cor. 9:15).

• GOD'S GOAL—to bring Rambhau into the family of God.
• THE PROCESS—missionary Morris must win Rambau by love and patiently wait for his eyes to be opened to see God's Gift.
• THE TIMING—only God could know what crisis it would take to unveil God's grace to Rambhau's heart.

FATHER, it is Your mercy and grace that finally opens blinded eyes to see and accept. Your goal had been reached! For the missionary the process had seemed long, yet now he could announce: it was worth it all.

Modeling God's Character

COSTA DEIR WRITES:
A TEACHER, (whom we will call Sandra) while reading an article from another country, recognized a need in that foreign school for the subjects that were her specialty. She applied for the position and was accepted. She had always wanted to be a witness for the Lord in her profession, especially in a nation where she could present the Christian message. She felt assured this was her opportunity.

The first day Sandra arrived, she met the principal who explained that her qualifications were acceptable and they would like to have a contract for two years. When she began to fill out the contract the principal said, "Before you sign the contract, I would like to ask you a private question." He asked, "What is your religion?" She, replied, "I am a born-again Christian."

He said,"We are not Christians here and we want to ask you not to mention anything about Christ as long as you are a teacher in this school." She responded to him, "Thank you for letting me know your requirements, for if that is your policy, I can't sign the contract. I will leave today for home." He was shocked. But she was determined that she could not accept these restrictions nor teach there. He begged her to go to the hotel that night, meditate on his request and come back the next morning with her answer.

She agreed to do as he had asked. She spent most of the night praying, and asking the Lord to speak to her heart. She was brokenhearted, "Lord, I have spent much money to come here with the intent of witnessing to Your saving grace. Now, I cannot do it." The Lord said to her, "In your country you talked about Me. Here, in this country, let your life be lived in such a way that My life will shine through you. It costs less to preach the gospel than to live the gospel. Remember, I came to serve, not to be served. Be a servant to these people and model the gospel to them."

Sandra went back to the principal the next morning, signed the contract, and agreed to say nothing. As she was praying, God led her to volunteer to tutor the worst students in the school. She began to minister to them one by one. They were known for being lazy, disruptive, vulgar, and they had no initiative. However, through her loving ministry, little by little, the worst of them became the best in the school.

As word of her ability spread to the families of all the students, Sandra could hardly cope with the number of invitations to visit the homes of students and tutor them. At the end of her two-year contract she was greatly appreciated, really loved, and accepted in their culture.

On the last day of school, she met with the principal. She thanked him for the opportunity of being with them and asked for her passport to be returned because she would be leaving the following day. He refused to give her the passport. He said that the parents of the students had a special meeting. They called him to advise him never to give this teacher her passport, even though this was the custom after the contract expired. But in her case, they insisted she should stay as long as she lives, because she had proven to be such a loving person who had served these people untiringly.

Sandra explained to him, "I will promise to come back. However, I must at least visit my family for six months." When she promised to come back, he agreed to return her passport. She realized that God had given her very special grace in his sight and in the sight of the people.

She then dared to ask the principal, "Since this is my last day in school, would you permit me to talk about my Jesus?"

"Oh!" he replied, "you may talk about Him all day today." He never realized what impact one day could make on the students. Who can understand the power of the Holy Spirit? She was so excited, she hurried to her apartment, exchanged the textbooks for her Bible, and came back to school rejoicing in the Lord.

All that day she traveled from Genesis to Revelation in the Bible, preaching without any restrictions. At the end of the day she asked the school students: "Now you have heard all about my Jesus. How many of you would like to be like Him and accept Him as your Savior?"

Many of their hands went up. Sitting immediately before her, in the first row, were the worst students that she had helped. They had become top students in their class. One of them who was especially unbearable, had terrified all the students. She had hoped that he and the rest of his gang would raise their hands. None of them responded because they were waiting for his move. Yet, there was a steady stream of tears coming down his face.

She asked him, "Don't you want to become like Jesus?" "No, I don't know who Jesus is... all this time I have wanted to be like you."

"Oh!" she exclaimed, "I am like Jesus."

At once he announced, "Oh, if you are like Jesus, then I want to be like Jesus." He really meant it! Not only did He, but all his gang received Christ as their personal Savior. Can you imagine the joy that flooded her heart at the end of that day. (C.D.)

Again we recognize God's GOAL, PROCESS AND TIMING Sandra had been convinced that God's goal was to share the gospel with these people. But like missionary Morse, she also needed to better understand God's process and His timing. As missionary Morse had spent years of planting and watering the Seed, so Sandra must patiently plant and water for two years.

I wonder if you have painfully discovered that "serving others" has turned out to be much different than you anticipated. No one ever explained to you that there would be so much laying aside your comforts, and patient modeling if you expected to be fruitful for Him. You have been so immersed in expecting "instant processing" that you want to claim "instant conversions."

FATHER, I thank You for setting me free from any illusions I've had about Christian service. I would surely have packed my bags and headed home, when I discovered I could not "teach in my way, as I had expected." Like Sandra, let me learn the first rule of serving: is to keep listening for Your directions, and then to be as adjustable clay in Your hands. I do recognize that all along the highways of Christian service the ditches are filled with folk who didn't listen and couldn't adjust. They couldn't accept Your process and wholly TRUST Your timing. Please, do not let me become a castaway... from Your purposes!

"Each one should use whatever gift he has received to serve others, faithfully administering God's grace in its various forms... If anyone serves, he should do it with the strength God provides, so that in all things God may be praised through Jesus Christ. To Him be the glory and the power for ever..."

The Auction

SOME YEARS AGO WHILE VISITING. . . in England, I found this story. It so caught my attention I have been attempting to verify it, and only recently I discovered it actually happened in this manner: Back in the days of the second World War, one of the wealthiest men in the United Kingdom, and his only son shared a passion for art collecting. They traveled around the world, adding only the finest art treasures to their collection. The widowed father took great delight in his son, because he had developed such a skill as an art collector.

When the war engulfed the nation, the young son felt the need to serve his country so he entered the service but it was for only a few months. The young son was killed while rushing a fellow soldier to a medic. Anguish and sadness filled the father's heart until one Christmas morning when he answered the door. There stood a soldier holding a large package, who greeted him, "I was a friend of your son, in fact I was the one he was rescuing when he was killed. I have something I would like to show you, may I come in?"

He told the father how his son had often explained how much they loved the priceless works of art they had collected, and the soldier who stood before him announced, "I am an artist; I want to give you this portrait I have painted of your son to show my appreciation for his bravery in saving my life."

Overcome with emotion, the father thanked the soldier for the portrait and promised to hang it above the fireplace where it would have the central attention. Of course no one would ever consider it the work of a genius, like others of his art collection, yet in the weeks and months that followed the father was to discover that, through the bravery of his son, dozens of wounded soldiers had been rescued before a bullet had stilled his caring heart.

As the stories of his son's gallantry continued to reach him, fatherly pride and satisfaction began to ease the grief, and the painting of his son became the prized possession, far eclipsing any interest in the other art pieces for which museums around the world clamored.

Shortly the old man died and the art world was in much anticipation. Unmindful of the story of the man's only son, but in his honor, the entire art collection was to be sold at auction on Christmas Day, because it was on that day the father had received his greatest gift: the portrait of his only son.

As the day arrived and art collectors from around the world gathered to bid on some of the world's spectacular paintings, the auction began with a painting that was not on any museum's list.

It was the painting of this man's son. It was the father's one stipulation! So, the auctioneer asked for an opening bid. The room was silent. "Who will open the bidding?" The room was silent, until a voice from the back of the room announced, "Who cares about that painting? Let's get on with the good stuff." More voices echoed agreement.

"No, we have to sell this one first," replied the auctioneer. There it stood on a tripod before all the crowd to consider. "Now, who will take this portrait of the son?" the auctioneer continued.

Nobody in the audience knew of the son, or really cared, for the painting was by an artist that nobody knew. To that crowd his portrait seemed almost valueless—something needing to be disposed of so they could get on with the most important business of the day.

Now there happened to be in the audience that day one of the family's life-time servants, who had known the boy and watched him grow up as he attended the family. He reflected on the many by-gone days when he had cared for the son. He thought to himself, how nice it would be to have this portrait as a remembrance. So he asked. "Will you take ten dollars for the painting? That's all I have. I knew the boy, so I'd like to have it."

"I have a ten dollar bid. Will anyone go higher?" called the auctioneer. After more silence, the auctioneer said, "Going once, going twice, Gone."

The gavel fell. Cheers filled the room as they waited for the auctioneer to proceed with further bids on the remaining treasures. But instead he announced in a stern voice: "Ladies and gentlemen, the auction is over!"

Everyone sat stunned! What in the world was happening? The auctioneer continued to read: "The will further stipulates that whoever gets the portrait of the son, get the whole lot. The entire art collection goes to this man here." He pointed to the old servant who stood admiring the picture he had just purchased.

What an angry crowd left that day! Yet each could only admit he had had the same opportunity as the faithful servant. What did this unusual demonstration really mean? This father was showing his deepest affection and honoring his only son.

There is Another Father who has a similar affection for His Son. You know I am speaking of our Heavenly Father's affection for His Son, the Lord Jesus. Since that single day on Calvary, our Father has made this question His central issue: what do you think of My Son?

Perhaps what is even more important is, (not what we think) but what does the Father think of His Son? To really understand this question, we must turn to Paul's explanation of the Father's plan and purpose long before he even started His creation program:

For God has allowed us to know the secret of His Plan, and it is this: He purposes in His sovereign will that all human history shall be consummated in Christ, that everything that exists in Heaven or earth shall find its perfection and fulfillment in Him. And here is the staggering thing—that in all which will one day belong to Him, we have been promised a share (since we were long ago destined for this by the One Who achieves His purposes by His sovereign will) so that we, as the first to put our confidence in Christ, may bring praise to His glory! (Eph. 1:10 Phillips Tr.)

Imagine! From the beginning, our Father had planned for His Son to be the Centerpiece of the universe. This was the original plan before creation and before Man's fall, that His Son—and those who comprise His Body–should have this glorious place of pre-eminence!...Yes, Paul continues: "The purpose is that all the angelic powers should now see the complex wisdom of God's plan being worked out through the Church, in conformity to that timeless Purpose which HE CENTERED IN JESUS OUR LORD.

FATHER, it is very possible that millions will be just as surprised as that audience in that final day... when the curtain is pulled back... and they discover the Father has planned for His Son, Christ Jesus, to be honored as His Centerpiece. I pray that none who read this will be angry, or be like that surprised crowd!

Jessie... Prisoner of Hope

JESSIE MILLER WRITES:

First, Second, Third squad—all present.

OUR nerves were tense. Why did this have to happen? Had one man really taken off? "Oh, God be merciful. If possible please put a little love in the hearts of these guards."
Fourth squad—all present.
As the bongo (roll call) progressed, my heart pounded fearfully. I knew the penalty we would pay if one man was missing. It would mean death for all the rest of us in our squad. All of us had seen death in every way, shape and form. We had been forced to watch many of our comrades die on that horrible death march from the tip of Bataan Peninsula to Camp O'Donnell.

We had listened carefully to the choppy orders from our captors: "Do not escape or you will be shot to death." Too many died there without any attempt to escape.

After a time, many of us were marched off to Camp Cabanatuan. All of it was enclosed by an 8-foot high barbed-wire fence, interspersed with frequent guardhouses from which the enemy kept an eagle eye on us. I noticed that a certain area had three rows of these tall fences.

Even so, due to severe mistreatment, some persons would try to escape. To do so endangered the rest of us. Every prisoner was assigned to a ten-man group. My barracks housed a hundred prisoners, so there were ten squads in our one barracks. With great apprehension we waited for Squad Nine to report.
Fifth, sixth, seventh squads—all present.
The roll call came closer. The finger of death was pointed at us. "Oh God, not us! Not me!"

Suddenly, my heart was quieted. I experienced the *"peace of God which passes all understanding."* It seemed strange to have peace and joy mixed in with tragedy.

I knew I had eternal life through my faith in Christ Jesus. No man could take that assurance from me. Just a year before enlisting in the Army Air Corps I had placed faith in the salvation the Lord Jesus Christ had provided. I believed that His death took the penalty of my sin. Words of assurance were great comfort to

200

me, *"He who hears My Word and believes on Him... is passed from death into Life"*. A deep and meaningful "Thank You, Lord" welled up within me.

I knew I was facing death at any moment. I wondered how the others in my squad were facing the same prospect. Did they know the peace which comes from receiving forgiveness and acceptance as a child of God?

Countless thoughts raced through my mind. I remembered Joe who died the first day the war reached us at Clark Field. Earlier in our friendship, he had told me of his longing for something more in life. He shared with me that this desire began when his sister explained in her letter that she had placed faith in Christ as her personal Savior and that joy and peace now filled her life. Joe asked me in all sincerity, "What can I do to be more fulfilled in my life?" Rings of fresh dirt showed on his trousers when we walked back to our barracks. In the days that followed Joe and I often met on a nearby hillside to pray and read about God.

Then suddenly, it was December 8! Clark Field was heavily bombed. The ambulance Joe was driving received a direct hit. Joe was taken from me.

The memory of Fred also flooded my thoughts. On the day war first reached us at Clark Field, we were a bunch of frightened young recruits, unprepared for war. In the midst of falling bombs, Fred, another buddy of mine, placed his faith in Christ. In the days of uncertainty, frustration and suffering which followed, peace controlled him. His panic was gone. He no longer carried the guilt of sins. This brought a strong bond between us. Even though we were prisoners, we sensed a freedom in Christ.

Three months later both Fred and I were among the 60,000 prisoners who were forced to step out on the infamous Death March from Bataan. Physical life ended for Fred when he dropped from exhaustion and received the dreaded "cold steel process" by the enemy's bayonet.

Ninth squad... one missing!!!

Now I was facing death. I thought I would soon be joining Joe and Fred. The longing to be with Christ was very strong. I knew that would be far better for me. But what about the other eight men who stood in line with me? Were they ready to die? At that strategic moment, I knew God was asking me if I was willing to tell each of them of Christ's salvation available to them.

"Oh yes, Lord, I am willing to do that and to go wherever You lead me, even back here to the Philippines or to the land of Japan." I meant that with all my heart.

Immediately, I knew there would be no massacre. As determined as our captors were to squeeze the triggers, they could not. It was God Who intervened. There was no slaughter. The enemy officer commanded us to return to our barracks and ordered us to be prepared for the shooting the next morning. That evening I witnessed personally to every man in squad nine of Christ's substitutionary death for them. Each man was left with his own accountability to God.

The next morning, there was no firing line to face. We were ordered back to work. Most of us went back to slave labor in the fields, and others to their work on airfield construction for the enemy.

As I thought of the miracle that had taken place, I realized it was God's mercy which had kept me from a bomb hit; He had supplied strength to make the Death March; I had not starved nor succumbed to severe fevers. **Repeatedly my life had been spared**. Why? **What purpose did God have** for me? Again, I resolved I would follow Him wherever He would lead. (JM)

Jesse was spared because God had plans which were about to unfold. Three and a half years later, at war's end Jessie arrived home safely, and after completing his studies at Biola he headed for the Far East. While in route to the Philippines, the Lord blessed Jessie with a wife, Nettie Dyk, a missionary in Tokyo. This union was greatly blessed by God, and the Millers with their family were led to open their home to American service men.

After much prayer Jessie and Nettie determined that God was leading them to birth an organization, (OCSC), dedicated solely to reaching military people for Christ. Throughout the next 46 years Overseas Christian Servicemen's Centers established in many corners of the world have continued to demonstrate what God can do through one man and his wife who have wholly surrendered themselves to fulfilling God's purpose. What a blessing for a couple to know the peace of God, but that was not enough. Jessie and Nettie were to become channels for sharing the gospel of peace with many others.

No, I Don't Want Any!

DR. SWIHART WRITES:

A LONG TIME AGO. . .
in my first writing venture, I produced twelve tiny pamphlets on the Christian faith, releasing one issue per month. Once I took a stack of these booklets to a Christian doctor, hoping to interest him to buy a dozen copies, and to leave them on his counter. Before I could speak with him, I had to wait some time in his waiting room. This was a good time to practice my sales presentation. I rehearsed my speech until I felt assured he would buy some books.

Finally, he came in and sat down in front of me. 'I was ready,' my self-confidence was vainly telling me. The doctor listened to my passionate presentation.

"I have just one question for you," he asked. "Why are you writing this material?"

That was easy enough, I thought. If that was his only concern, then I was in good shape. I proceeded to tell him about my urgent desire to see Christians become mature. I explained how my material was carefully designed to help believers grow spiritually.

"That's the wrong answer," he bluntly said at the end of my defense. "I don't want any of your booklets!"

I was shocked! When he said I had given 'the wrong answer,' I felt as though a powerful electrical current was attacking my whole body. 'How could my reply possibly be incorrect,' I thought. In bold disbelief, I asked the doctor what he meant; what answer should I have given?

What he told me, nearly thirty years ago, has stuck with me like a battle scar.

"The only thing I wanted to hear you say," he said, "was that God was leading you to write this literature. What *you* want to do, even for Christians, is of no interest to me. But if you told me that God had planted this project in your heart; then I would have bought all of your books.

Immediately, I explained to him how his basic point went without saying. It was a given.

"If God tells you to do something," he said, interrupting me at that point, "it cannot go *without saying*. In fact, it must be the first and the primary thing you say."

With that, he got up, dismissed me, and sent me home like a puppy with my tail between my legs.

There was a deep lesson in this for me to learn from this Christian doctor. My service for God must not be primarily motivated by the needs I witness in others. Or even by the desires in my own heart. Instead, my work must be the distinct response to the leading of the Holy Spirit. Self-styled service, even for the Lord Himself, is unacceptable. What I do for Him, first and foremost, must be a response to the passion He Himself plants in my heart. God is not seeking volunteers to work for Him, however it pleases *them*. Rather, He is looking for submissive people to serve Him however it pleases *Him!* (S.S.)

The real service is not doing work, the real service is serving God's will. We must realize service does not have its emphasis on the work we do, but on the will of God.

Today, many people evaluate our earthly profession by job performance. As to the character of the worker, it is secondary. Yet in God's sight, His interest is not so much on doing the work, but rather on how we serve His will.

Father, it becomes more obvious all along, that my daily hearing Your voice is the only sure way I can serve Your will. I can see needs all around me; I can hear many calls for help, but I now realize You are the one who "sends forth labors into the field." "As they ministered to the Lord... the Holy Spirit said... Separate me Barnabas and Saul for the work whereunto I have called them... so they being sent forth by the Holy Spirit..."
To be called is one thing; to be sent is another.

Duan's Christmas Miracle

IT WAS AN ALMOST. . . unbelievable miracle that happened to Brother Duan, but he would not have experienced it had the bus he was riding not broken down. En route from a northern to a southern province of China in December, he happened to be passing through Henan province when the engine of the bus expired in its futile battle with the cold.

On a whim, Duan trudged off through the fields, leaving the other passengers huddled inside the bus. He was a house church leader in northern China. Now 77 years of age, he moved continually from church to church and had no home to call his own.

Truth is, he was deeply depressed. He was on his way to mediate a dispute among some leaders and was weary of the infighting that seemed to be harming the house churches. Moreover he was lonely!

As he crossed the frozen field, Duan thought longingly of his beloved wife, who died long ago. He wished she were alive to listen to him and give her sweet counsel. And then the thought came into his tired mind of his little son, and an even darker cloud settled over his aching heart.

He arrived at a small village and knocked on a door. He observed a little cross was notched on the doorpost.

"Is there anyone here who loves the Lord?" he asked. "I would enjoy some fellowship tonight." The door was opened by a man in his fifties, and Duan was warmly welcomed. His feet were washed in a basin—the custom of welcoming a stranger among the house church movement—and he was fed hot congee and steaming vegetables.

He noticed that the people were all excited. They explained that they would be traveling to a neighboring town to hear an unusual Bible teacher from one of the bigger cities.

"What's his name?" asked Duan.

"Brother Wang."

They encouraged him to go with them. As they made their way to the meeting, they told him some of the stories about this mysterious Brother Wang. It was clear they loved him dearly, and one of the men explained why.

"We were once holding a training seminar here and heard the police were coming. Brother Wang got everyone out, except our main pastor. When the police arrived, Wang dared to bargain with them. He would go to jail if their pastor—whose wife was eight months pregnant—could go free. The policeman accepted the terms, and Brother Wang spent three years in prison.

How old is Brother Wang?" Duan asked. When they explained he was in his early 40's, Duan's showed great pain.

"What's the matter?" he was asked. "Are you ill from the cart trip?"

"No, I'm not ill," he replied, "just very sad. I once had a son, whom I knew for just two months. He's dead now, but if he were alive he would have been 42 today.

"My wife called him the Christmas child, since he was born at Christmas time. I called him 'Isaac,' because we had despaired for so long of having a child."

There was a silence as they rode in the open cart under the stars. Brother Duan told the incredible story of how he and his wife had been evangelists in the 1950's. They refused to join the Three Self Church. Wu, an old school bully, kept accusing them of political and criminal offenses. They realized it was only a matter of time before they would be jailed or killed; then what would happen to their boy?

One night, Duan's wife heard a strong voice in a vision, saying, "Give your son to your enemy." Knowing nothing of this, Duan read Genesis 22:2 the following morning: "Go get Isaac, your only son, the one you dearly love... and sacrifice him to me."

Sharing their impressions, the couple decided on a course of action that caused Duan to wince in pain every day since. They decided to give their boy to Wu and his wife—who were child-less—even as Wu was arranging for the couple's arrest.

It was years later when Duan was released from jail, that he learned what happened to his wife and son. She had died in a terrible famine, and his son had disappeared along with the Wu family under the rubble of a devastating earthquake. Said Duan sadly as the cart approached the meeting place, "God judged me for being so irresponsible with my little son."

As they arrived where the evangelist was to speak, a crowd of 200 people was already packed into the house. Like many others, Duan had to sit in the courtyard and listen to the teacher through the open window.

When Brother Wang began preaching, Duan felt a terrible shock. It was like hearing himself. He began to tremble with fear. Was he dying? Even the phrases the teacher used sounded familiar.

Confused, he staggered up to the window to see the preacher, causing a commotion as he fell over people. The preacher stopped and there was a moment of shocked silence as the men looked at each other. The crowd was hushed as they realized the amazing physical likeness.

"I'm sorry for interrupting your excellent message," Duan began. "You see, I had a son who would be your age right now. If he had lived, he would have looked and sounded just like you."

Brother Wang began to tremble violently. Suddenly, his legs buckled under him and he had to be caught before he fell. Clutching his pounding chest, he sobbed out, "Are you Daddy Duan?"

Everyone wept as father and son were reunited. The preacher told how he had indeed been brought up by Wu, who was so impressed by Duan's act of giving that he had trusted Christ and become a strong Christian.

"I'm not your real father," Wu used to say to him. "He's a great man of God, full of grace and love. He gave you to me, and I give you all my love and the encouragement to put God first, just like your real father."

Wang's adoptive parents had moved away from the earthquake zone before the tragedy, however both had died of cancer in their 60's. When Wang became an evangelist, he spent much time trying to find his real father, but Duan had changed his name so many times to avoid arrest he had proved untraceable.

As father and son continued to hug and weep, the elder of the church stood up and declared, "It's Christmas! We have seen our sermon tonight: Christ came into the world to save sinners-that is Christmas. Just as Duan handed his only son to the care of his enemy, so God handed His own Son up for us sinners. Let us rejoice in their reunion and our blessings tonight."

Again, we see how God is writing the last chapter. When He asks for our obedience, sometimes it is beyond our comprehension. How could such "work out for good... according to his purpose?" Surely it was in the foreknowledge of God that He could ask them to give their son.

And finally it is the goodness of Father/God that He directs Duan away from that stalled bus and then to attend that meeting "at that appointed time."

We have been saying that God's will involves these three aspects: the goal, the process and the timing. We often assume that we know God's goal and now must discover the process and timing. But in this story of Duan, we see the difficult process long before God's goal or His timing are made clear.

What was the process? God asks Duan and his wife to give their son to an enemy. How could they know this was the way God would spare the baby from death and make a mighty servant for the house church movement. In His foreknowledge, God was working toward a goal—not yet known to Duan. All He is asking from them is simple obedience. We often refer to "yielding... as our intelligent service"; but in this instance it is their blind obedience that unfolds the will of God. We must never forget, God does not expect us to always understand His ways—but simply to know that He is TRUSTworthy.

* Consider how God alone knew His goal and His timing for Joseph to become the "economic savior" of Egypt during a famine.

* Consider how Moses spent 40 years of preparation in the dessert before he was ready to deliver God's people from Egypt.

* Consider how David herded his father's sheep for 30 years before he was crowned king by all the tribes of Israel.

* Consider the long PROCESS that had been working in the life of Abraham before he would become the father of many nations. Did Abraham understand this PROCESS when God asked him to sacrifice his son, Isaac? Perhaps you have been asking how a loving Father could ask Duan and his wife to give up their son; or you have pondered how God could ask Abraham to give up His son, Isaac. Let me remind you that Father/God has never asked anything of us—that He Himself has not already done in giving His Son to die on the cross.

FATHER, I hear You asking me to TRUST you even when I cannot understand Your Goal or timing. In Your ways I see the pattern unfolding!

"What shall we then say to these things?... He that spared not His own son, but delivered him up for us all, how shall he not with him also freely give us all things?... and his ways past finding out!" (Rom. 8:31-32)

Rachel's Tears

ALL THE NATION
was shocked as the TV cameras focused on the unfolding story of
Columbine High School. When the final count revealed thirteen
dead from the shooting by two students, everyone questioned
why! What good could possibly come from this carnage? Even
more amazing was the full coverage by CNN of the funeral of
Rachel Scott, one of the girls who had died for her Christian witness. T.V. sources disclosed later this funeral had an even greater
audience than that of Princess Diana a few months earlier.

Surely God has been speaking to everyone, especially the
youth of our nation! And more recently now, the twin-tower and
Pentagon carnage. What is God saying to all of us? I needed some
answers, so I read through two books which covered the life-story
of two girls who had been brutally killed in the Columbine
shooting.

One of the books, Rachel's Tears, written by her mother and
her father, unfolded the struggle of their daughter to find spiritual meaning and peace with God amidst the turmoil of school life
in the halls of Columbine. In her journal Rachel had written many
revealing bits and pieces which exposed her honesty toward God,
and her search for strength to overcome temptations. Now, the
whole nation has looked into her heart and every one of us
admired her brutal transparency and her intense longing to know
and please God.

Just recently when I answered my phone, I was excited to
hear the voice of her father. "This is Darrell Scott calling; I am the
father of Rachel Scott, who was killed in...!" I was not only excited
but most honored to receive his call regarding his coming visit
to Indianapolis. His voice revealed a man who had experienced
the peace of God, but even more (as the book reveals), Darrell has
become a man gripped by a sense of destiny and purpose. He has
become increasingly determined that his daughter's death should
not be in vain, but shall start a chain reaction: Darrell Scott
explains his story:

"I woke up at 4:30 one morning about a month after Rachel's
funeral... and two scriptures from the Bible were ringing in my
mind... as though God was speaking to me:

"I have brought you to the kingdom for such a time as this."
"I will put you before kings and leaders and you will
not be afraid of what to say, I will put words in your mouth."

What seemed so unlikely then has come to reality. Many opportunities continue to open for Darrell to speak (not only to our Congress) but to large audiences throughout this nation and abroad.

He continues, "Several days after this experience of sensing God speaking to me... one morning I prayed out loud: 'God, I want to do whatever You are calling me to do, but I have two requests. I do not want to open doors for speaking... and I don't want to wear suits. I prefer comfortable clothes."

"Within ten minutes of that prayer, the phone rang. It was a man... who had seen Rachel's funeral. He said the Lord had shown him that I was going to be raised up to speak to leaders and young people all across this country... he wanted to lend his financial support to whatever God was calling me to do... What he said next was to become a major contribution to Rachel's testimony. He (explained that he had) dreamed (shortly after Rachel's funeral) about her eyes and tears that were watering something that he couldn't quite see in the dream. He was perplexed about the eyes and tears, and wanted to know if that meant anything to me. He was disappointed when I said, "No... I don't have any idea what that means." Then he explained that the dream had haunted him for days, and he knew there was a reason for it... and asked me to call him if I could ever shed light on what he felt was a true vision from God.

"Several days later... they released Rachel's backpack that she had on when she was murdered...We suspected that Rachel's final diary was still in the backpack... there were two of them. One of them had a bullet hole entering at a place on the back cover where she had written the words 'I WON'T BE LABELED AS AVERAGE.' I wept uncontrollably as I read what she had written on the front cover: "I write, not for the sake of glory, not for the sake of fame, nor for the sake of success, but for the sake of my soul— Rachel Joy."

"Could Rachel have ever suspected... within months that her written words would be heard around the world? That they would be quoted by newscasters across the nation? That they would be printed in book form for the reading of generations of young people yet to be born? But my biggest shock was yet to come!

I turned to the end of her last diary and could not believe what was staring up at me from the final page! A drawing of her eyes with a stream of tears that were watering a rose! Later someone pointed out that there were thirteen clear tears falling from her eyes before they touched the rose and turned into what looked like blood drops. There were, of course, thirteen victims of the two murderers. I was so stunned that I could barely breathe.

"Imagine! A week ago a complete stranger phoned, who lived more than a thousand miles away. He had described exactly what I was looking at in Rachel's final diary! I prayed for God to help me understand what was happening... we discovered that same rose in a previous diary drawn a year before Rachel's death. The first drawing also showed the rose growing up out of a columbine plant. Columbine High School got its name from the state flower. In addition to that, she had drawn a cross with the words: *"Greater love hath no man than this, that a man would lay down his life for his friends"!*

"We had two drawings a year apart that form a total picture! A scripture... beside that verse is a columbine flower, out of which is growing a rose that is being watered by drops of blood that have as their source thirteen clear teardrops from the eyes of a young girl named Rachel.

"I believe... the Columbine tragedy was a spiritual wake-up call to the youth of this generation. This one story that has had the most impact on the youth... is the story of the rose.

"Several weeks after I first saw Rachel's drawing, a young girl (in Jackson, Tenn. where I was speaking) came up to me sobbing.

She said, "Mr Scott, I did not know what you were going to talk about before you came, but I had felt impressed to have you read some verses from the Bible. Then she handed me her Bible (which was) opened to Jer. 31:15-17 NIV: This is what the Lord says:

"A voice is heard in Ramah, mourning and great weeping,
Rachel weeping for her children;
and refusing to be comforted, because they are no more...
Restrain your voice from weeping,
and your eyes from tears, for your work shall be rewarded..."

"When I read those words, the door of closure slammed shut in my spirit. I knew from that moment that Rachel's death was not in vain. I knew that this teacher and twelve students were going to have an eternal impact on the lives of many people... This tragedy would be turned into triumph by the grace of God!" (D.S.)

It Is Too Soon to Evaluate

IN 1921, A MISSIONARY couple named David and Svea Flood traveled with their two-year-old son from Sweden to the Belgian Congo in the heart of Africa. They joined another young Scandinavian couple, the Ericksons, and felt led of God to leave the main station and take the gospel to a remote area. This was a real step of faith.

At the village of N'dolera the chief would not let them enter his town for fear of alienating the local gods, so the two couples went half a mile up the slope and built their own mud huts. They prayed for a spiritual breakthrough, but there was none.

The only contact with the villagers was a young boy who sold them chickens and eggs twice a week. Svea Flood—only four feet, eight inches tall—decided that if this was the only African she could talk to, she would try to lead the boy to Jesus. She succeeded, but there were no other encouragements.

Malaria struck one member of the little band after another and in time the Ericksons decided to return to the mission station, leaving their friends to go on alone. Then Svea became pregnant. When the time came for her to give birth, the village chief softened enough to allow a mid-wife to help her. A little girl was born, but the delivery was exhausting for Svea who was already weak from bouts of malaria. She lived only another seventeen days.

Something snapped inside David Flood. He dug a crude grave, buried his twenty-seven-year old wife, and then took his children back down the mountain. Handing his newborn daughter, Aina, to the Ericksons he snarled, "I'm going back to Sweden. I've lost my wife and I can't take care of this baby. God has ruined my life."

With that, he headed for the port, rejecting not only his calling, but his God. Within eight months both the Ericksons were stricken ill and died within days of each other. The baby was turned over to some American missionaries who adjusted her Swedish name to "Aggie" and eventually brought her back to the United States. They decided to stay in their home country and switch from missionary work to pastoral ministry and that is how Aggie grew up in South Dakota.

As a young woman, she attended Bible College where she met and married a young man named Dewey Hurst. Years passed and in time Aggie's husband became president of a Christian college in the Seattle area where there was a strong Scandinavian heritage. One day a Swedish religious magazine appeared in her mailbox. She had no idea who had sent it, and couldn't read the words, but as she turned the pages, all of a sudden a photo stopped her cold. There in a primitive setting was a grave with a white cross—and on the cross were the words SVEA FLOOD. Aggie found a college faculty member who could translate the article and explain what it said.

The instructor summarized the story of missionaries who had come to N'dolera long ago, the birth of a white baby, the death of the young mother, the one little African boy who had been led to Christ, and how he had grown up and finally persuaded the chief to let him build a school in the village. Gradually he won all his students to Christ and the children led their parents to Christ, even the chief. Amazing ! Today there were six hundred Christian believers in that one village—all because of the sacrifice of David and Svea Flood.

For the Hursts' twenty-fifth wedding anniversary, the college sent them on a vacation to Sweden where Aggie sought out her real father. An old man now, David Flood had remarried, fathered four more children, and generally dissipated his life with alcohol. He had recently suffered a stroke. Still bitter, he had one rule in his family: "Never mention the name of God—because God took everything from me."

After an emotional reunion with her step-family, Aggie went to see her father. She walked into the squalid apartment littered with liquor bottles and approached the seventy-three-year-old man lying in a rumpled bed. "Papa?" she said tentatively.

He turned and began to cry, "Aina," he said, "I never meant to give you away."

"It's all right, Papa," she replied, hugging him gently. "God took care of me."

The man instantly stiffened. The tears stopped. "God forgot all of us. Our lives have been like this because of Him." He turned his face to the wall but Aggie continued undaunted.

"Papa, you didn't go to Africa in vain. Mamma didn't die in vain. The little boy you led to the Lord won that whole village to Jesus. The seed you planted just kept growing and growing.

Today six hundred Africans are serving the Lord because you were faithful to the call of God. Papa, Jesus loves you. He never hated you."

The old man turned back to look into his daughter's eyes. His body relaxed and by the end of the afternoon David Flood had come back to the God he had resented for so many decades.

A few years later at an evangelism conference in London, the Hursts listened to a report from the nation of Zaire (the former Belgian Congo). The superintendent of the national church, representing 110,000 baptized believers, spoke eloquently of the gospel's spread in his nation. Aggie approached him afterwards and asked if he had ever heard of David and Svea Flood.

"Yes, mame," the man replied, "It was Svea who led me to Christ. I was the boy who brought food to your parents before you were born. In fact, to this day your mother's grave and her memory are honored by all of us." He embraced her in a long, sobbing hug and then said, "You must come to Africa to see, because your mother is the most famous person in our history."

And that is exactly what Aggie Hurst and her husband did. They were welcomed by cheering throngs of villagers as the pastor escorted Aggie to her mother's white cross where she knelt and gave thanks. Later that day in the church, the pastor read from John 12:24: *"I tell you the truth, unless a kernel of wheat falls to the ground and dies, it remains only a single seed. But if it dies, it produces many seeds."* He followed with Psalm 126:5: *"Those who sow in tears will reap with songs of joy..."* (Jim Cymbala)

It is always too soon to evaluate any life and ministry. Consider how the Lord sovereignly arranged for Aggie to receive that magazine, to meet her father and help restore him to faith. What a wonderful gift from the Lord for Aggie to recognize God's blessings through her family and for all the African converts to have opportunity to express their appreciation. God's goal, process and timing are so evident in this story. What a fitting word as we close this book! Yes, God alone unveils all the unknown issues in any life... and He will reward in His time.

In reflecting back, I remember the five years of ministry my dear wife, Nita, had in India before we were married. And I also recall the deep sighing of her heart as we prayed often for those she had touched during her years in India. She may have left India, but she never left her house-boy, Chintaman, who trusted Christ, and so faithfully served her, or another 17 year-old girl, Sushila, who was rescued from sin and an arranged marriage. There were scores of others who came together for a girls retreat whose lives were impacted. by her life. Who knows! Only eternity will reveal what God has done through her poured-out life unto Him!.

It is to this end, I feel it is appropriate for us to pay this tribute

TO NITA... LOVED BY GOD... AND HER FAMILY.
IN HER HONOR AND REMEMBRANCE, WE
DEDICATE THIS BOOK... AND TO THE MANY
WHO READ AND FOLLOW THE EXHORTATIONS
IN THESE PAGES.

For their devoted help in preparing this manuscript
I am indebted to...
Bill Mallon for his initial planning
Kris Peterson for her layout and type preparation
Ruth Cowart for her final editing and proofreading.

Some of these stories date back over 50 years when I first started collecting illustrations. If I had been planning for publication, I would have used greater care in establishing authorship and ownership so I could obtain permission and grant credit for the origin. Please grant mercy and help us establish ownership and we'll give proper acknowledgement in future editions. We will accept your true stories for another book, if you give the author's name and original source of story if previously published.

ACKNOWLEDGEMENTS

God Knows Your Number... by Kenneth Gaub from book: GOD KNOWS YOUR NUMBER.

God Knows Your Blindness... by Billy Graham, his newsletter.

I Don't Believe There Is A God... by Watchman Nee from, WHAT SHALL THIS MAN DO. Published by Christian Literature Crusade.

The Bible Can Do More... by John MacArthur from; OUR SUFFICIENCY IN CHRIST. Word Publishing, Dallas, TX.

Hearing God For Life... by Peter Lord in book: HEARING GOD. Order from: Dunklin Memorial Church, 3342 S.W. Hosannah Lane, Okeechobee, FL 34974.

Scripture Strengthens Prayer... by Edith Marshall in BREAKTHROUGH.

"Heavenly Currency" quote... by Norm Willis in VERTICAL REALITY. Order from Christ Church Publishing, 11725 NE 118th Ave., Kirkland, WA 98054.

In Beholding, We are Becoming... by Steve McVey in monthly GRACE newsletter

Conversion... by Frances Angermermayer in Our Sunday Visitor, Huntington, Indiana.

The Smell of Rain... by Diana and David Blessing used by their permission

God Was There... Betty, by David A Seamands in book, HEALING FOR DAMAGED EMOTIONS Victor Books, 1825 College Ave. Wheaton, IL.

A Song in the Night... story taken from EXPLOITS, magazine of Slavic Gospel Association.

Could You have Loved as Much?... by Bob Considine adapted and retold by author.

Extravagant Love... by J. David Newman in MINISTRY MAGAZINE.

Greatness In Disguise... by Lillian Harvey from ROYAL INSIGNIA order from Rt. 2, Box 368, Hampton, TN 37658.

The Whole Tree Was White—story has various sources, retold by author.

She's My Friend–unknown—published in various periodicals.

Why Uncle Left The Ministry by Marcia Barnard Chandler published in the 1984 FARMER'S ALMANAC.

Tools or Toys... by Jamie Buckingham; from Wycliff Translators.

Did He Do it Right? by Jamie Jett from a church bulletin.

The Love of the Father... author unknown, adapted from Daily Bread, Radio Bible Class.

Righteousness and Peace Kissed... illustration by Clay Sterrett, in BRINGING ANIMALS OF EVERY KIND INTO THE ARK. CFC Literature, P.O. Box 245, Staunton, VA.

Their Joy Was Missing. by Watchman Nee in TWELVE BASKETS FULL Hong Kong Church Bookroom.

Jessie... Prisoner of Hope... by Jessie Miller in NINE MUST DIE... Read the entire book: order from Nettie Miller, 2020 S. Deframe Way, Lakewood, CO 80228.

No I Don't Want Any... Dr. Stephen Swihart, story from his excellent Teaching Syllabus.

Rachel's Tears... by Beth Nimmo and Darrell Scott, this excerpt from the book: RACHEL'S TEARS published by Thomas Nelson Publishers, Nashville, TN.

It Is Too Soon to Evaluate... excerpt from an article SEEDS OF HOPE by Jim Cymbala with Dean Merrill—periodical: Servant/Spring 2001.

God-centered writings by DeVern Fromke available through Sure Foundation

Ultimate Intention

This classic has finally been reprinted and not a moment too soon! Every believer will be deeply impressed by a thorough reading of DeVern Fromke's classic setting forth the importance of God-centeredness for the normal Christian life. Beginning with an unfolding of God's eternal purpose which He purposed for Himself in eternity past, the various chapters set forth the importance of a God-centered view of reality as the only environment nurturing proper spiritual growth. It is not an exaggeration to say that this volume has radically altered many people's understanding of the Christian life, lifting it beyond the pale of "self-interest" and into the only realm it was intended to be lived—with God as Center! This new reprint includes a study guide and can be used for personal or group study. We highly recommend using it to spur spiritual growth in your church.

Life's Ultimate Privilege

Another important release from DeVern Fromke expressing the importance of prayer as the believer's ultimate privilege. From his rich storehouse of spiritual experience, the author provides personal accounts of answered prayer and draws from them application to encourage our own prayer life. This book will definitely challenge you to believe that of all the blessings which God has given us, surely prayer is the greatest. A great book for a prayerless life or church.

Unto Full Stature

Unto Full Stature describes a very practical outworking of ultimate truth. Anyone who has ever been gripped by the necessity and glory of living unto God for the realization of His ultimate intention cannot help but yearn for the more practical ways of fulfillment. This book attempts to lead each one step by step through eight levels or phases of our natural and spiritual maturity.

The author exposes hidden reasons why the child of God flounders in vision, lacks spiritual perspective, misunderstands his calling and purpose, disregards the important place of the will, and abuses his body as he zealously lives at exhaustion point.

A Hive of Busy Bees

Stories that build character for ages 5-10 by Effie Williams and others, compiled by DeVern Fromke. Don and Joyce are invited to spend the summer with their grandparents at the farm. Each day presents exciting opportunities for them to experience outdoor farm life—so different from the city—especially the first day when they encounter a hive of angry bees. From this episode Grandma chooses stories from her scrapbook and skillfully develops some character lessons for each evening bedtime BEE STORY. In the past sixty years, this all-time favorite book has been handed from parent to child to grandchild. All delight to hear the stories over and over again. It is amazing how many teachers have used the stories for closing the school week each Friday afternoon.

Another Hive of Bees

Stories that build character for ages 5-10 compiled by DeVern Fromke. Now a sequel in this series has been published through the cooperation of Christian school leaders and teachers who seek to provide Christ-honoring and character-building books for today's youth. Read how Danny and Debbie learn from, "Another Hive of Bees."

Seeing God's Wisdom

Seeing God's Wisdom is a collection of stories selected by DeVern Fromke that are intended to be read and discussed during family gathering time. Together you'll learn spiritual principles designed to build character.

Seeing God's Purpose

Like *Seeing God's Wisdom,* this collection of stories selected by DeVern Fromke are intended to be read and discussed during family gathering time. Together you'll learn spiritual principles about God's wisdom and how it can build character in your life.

To Order, Call or Write to:

Sure Foundation
8905 Kingston Pike Suite 12-316
Knoxville, TN 37923

Phone Orders Call Toll Free
1-800-325-9136
Local Calls and Fax Orders: 865-690-8161

Order on the web at either of these addresses:
http://www.surefoundation.com
http://www.master-press.com